1001
BIBLE TRIVIA QUESTIONS

BIBLEQUIZZES.ORG.UK

Contents Page

THE QUESTIONS

The Bible is a big book, but it's such an important book - it is a guide for our lives given to us by God, it is a *lamp unto our feet*. It is not always easy to read or understand, and the vast amount of information within its pages can certainly be overwhelming at times!

That's why we've created this book, to provide an entertaining way of helping you to discover more of the Bible and perhaps encouraging you to look more deeply into passages that interest you.

The questions are largely based on the King James Version of the Bible, but we have on occasions used other versions to give a better reading.

We've arranged the questions in order of difficulty, and while individual questions may be a little easier or harder than their position would suggest, each section as a whole gets progressively harder.

SECTION A

1. What was the name of Jesus' mother?
2. What was the name of the garden where Adam and Eve lived?
3. With what food did Jesus feed 5,000 people?
4. What method did the Romans use to kill Jesus?
5. From which part of Adam's body did God create Eve?
6. Who, when accused of being with Jesus, lied and said that he did not know him, three times?
7. Which creature tricked Eve into eating of the forbidden fruit?
8. At Christ's crucifixion what did the soldiers place on his head?
9. What is the first line of the *Lord's Prayer*?

10. What relationship was Ruth to Naomi?
11. Who lied to God when he was asked where his brother was?
12. Which Old Testament character showed his faith by being willing to offer his son on an altar to God?
13. What significant event is recorded in Genesis chapters 1 and 2?
14. What was inscribed above Jesus' cross?
15. Whose mother placed him in an ark of bulrushes?
16. For how many days and nights did it rain in the story of the flood?
17. What was special about Jesus' mother?
18. Who gave gifts to Jesus when he was a young child?
19. What happened to Jonah after he was thrown overboard?
20. In whose image was man created?

21. How many apostles did Jesus choose?
22. What are the wages of sin?
23. Who is the first mother mentioned in the Bible?
24. Who else, other than the wise men, came to visit Jesus when he was a small child?
25. Who lied when he was asked to reveal the source of his great strength?
26. What was the name of the man Jesus' mother was engaged to at the time she became pregnant?
27. Which book of the Bible records many of the hymns David wrote?
28. From what disaster did the Ark save Noah?
29. What happened to Jesus forty days after his resurrection?
30. What animals did Jesus cause to run into the sea and drown?
31. On what were the Ten Commandments written?
32. What did Jesus sleep in after he was born?
33. What was man created from?
34. What did Jesus do to each of the disciples during the Last Supper?
35. To which city did God ask Jonah to take his message?
36. Who was David's father?
37. Which of the gospels appears last in the Bible?
38. What is the only sin that cannot be forgiven?
39. How did David defeat Goliath?
40. What did Joseph's brothers do to get rid of him?
41. Who wrote the letter to Philemon?
42. In what was Jesus wrapped before he was buried?
43. What was the name of Moses' brother?
44. What sin is Cain remembered for?
45. "The Lord is my Shepherd," is the opening line to which Psalm?
46. What is the last book of the New Testament?
47. Who wrote the majority of the New Testament letters?
48. What was David's occupation before he became king?
49. Who hid two spies but claimed not to know of their whereabouts when asked?
50. Whose prayer resulted in his being thrown into a den of lions?

SECTION B

51. What was the apparent source of Samson's strength?

52. From which country did Moses help the Israelites escape from their lives of slavery?

53. Who was the fourth person in the fiery furnace along with Daniel's friends?

54. What did Joseph's brothers do to deceive their father to cover up that they had sold Joseph into slavery?

55. What kind of leaves did Adam and Eve sew together to make clothes for themselves?

56. Who did Jesus say was the "father of lies"?

57. What was the name of the tower that the people were building when God confused their language?

58. What is the common name of the prayer that Jesus taught to his disciples?

59. Whose name means "father of a great multitude"?

60. Of what did Potiphar's wife falsely accuse Joseph resulting in him being thrown into prison?

61. Which sea did the Israelites cross through to escape the Egyptians?

62. What is "more difficult than a camel going through the eye of a needle"?

63. For how many years did the Israelites wander in the wilderness?

64. What does a "good tree" bring forth?

65. Which small body part can "boast of great things"?

66. What was the name of Abraham's first wife?

67. What did God do on the seventh day, after he had finished creating everything?

68. On what day did the apostles receive the Holy Spirit?

69. At the Last Supper, what items of food and drink did Jesus give thanks for?

70. When Jesus was in the wilderness, what was he tempted to turn into loaves of bread?

71. What were the religious leaders called who continually tried to trap Jesus with their questions?

72. What miracle did Jesus do for Lazarus?

73. On which mountain were the Israelites given the Ten Commandments?

74. Who was Solomon's father?

75. What job did Jesus' earthly father, Joseph, do?

76. How did Judas betray Christ?

77. Solomon judged wisely over the rightful mother of a child, but how did he determine who the child belonged to?

78. Whose father was prepared to sacrifice him on an altar?

79. At the age of twelve, Jesus was left behind in Jerusalem. Where did his parents find him?

80. When the disciples saw Jesus walking on water, what did they think he was?

81. What gift did Salome, daughter of Herodias, ask for after she danced for Herod?

82. How did Samson kill all the people in the temple?

83. Which musical instrument did David play for Saul?

84. What was Esau doing while Jacob stole his blessing?

85. Why did Jacob initially send Joseph's brothers into Egypt?

86. Who was David's great friend?

87. Who said "thy God shall be my God"?

88. Which of Christ's belongings did the soldiers cast lots for after they had crucified him?

89. What does the name *Emmanuel* mean?

90. What does James say we should do if we lack wisdom?

91. Where did Jesus meet the woman of Samaria?

92. Which disciple tried to walk on water, as Jesus did?

93. Why did Elimelech go to live in Moab with his family?

94. Who lied about the price they received for a piece of land and died as a result?

95. With whom did David commit adultery?

96. When the Prodigal Son returned, his father gave him a robe, shoes and what other item?

97. How many books are there in the Bible?

98. What are the names of Lazarus' sisters?

99. Where did Jonah go after being thrown overboard and reaching dry land?

100. For what did Esau sell his birthright to Jacob?

SECTION C

101. What happened to Elimelech in Moab?

102. What does the shepherd in the parable of the lost sheep do once he realizes one is missing?

103. What is the name of the disciple who betrayed Jesus?

104. What golden animal did the Israelites make as an idol?

105. Who did Jesus appear to first after his resurrection?

106. What job did Peter and Andrew do?

107. Which prophet tried to flee from God when asked to preach God's message in Nineveh?

108. What is the collective name of the stories Jesus told to convey his message?

109. What was noticeable about Jacob's twin brother, Esau, at birth?

110. Who wanted to kill Jesus when he was a baby?

111. What did the earth look like in the beginning?

112. How did the father first respond upon seeing the Prodigal Son returning home?

113. Which well known Psalm of David contains the line, "he maketh me to lie down in green pastures"?

114. Abraham's wife, Sarah, bore a special son. What was his name?

115. Which son did Jacob love more than all the others?

116. Who was Jacob's grandfather?

117. To which city will all nations one day go to worship God?

118. Who said, "I am the true vine"?

119. When there was no water to drink in the wilderness, how did Moses provide it?

120. To which tribe did Jesus belong?

121. What tragedy did Jacob think had happened to Joseph?

122. What affliction did Hannah suffer from, that allowed Peninnah to provoke her?

123. Which is the gate that "leads to life"?

124. What happened to the man who built his house upon the sand?

125. What was the relationship of Mary (mother of Jesus) to Elisabeth?

126. How should we treat those who are our enemies, according to Jesus?

127. Who said, "Thou art my beloved Son, in thee I am well pleased"?

128. Which son did Jacob not send to Egypt for grain during the famine?

129. What does the word "gospel" mean?

130. Who suggested that Jonah be thrown overboard?

131. What did Ruth do to Boaz while he was sleeping?

132. As Esau grew, he was described as a *what...?*

133. When Jesus went to dinner at Simon the Pharisee's house, what did a woman do for him?

134. What was Bathsheba doing when David first saw her?

135. When the law was given to the children of Israel, what were they told not to worship?

136. Who ran from Mount Carmel to Samaria faster than Ahab could drive his chariot?

137. How many sons did Jacob (Israel) have?

138. Which disciple wanted to see the imprint of the nails before he would believe?

139. Which king dreamed about a large statue of a man made from different metals?

140. What form did the Holy Spirit take at the baptism of Jesus?

141. Complete the saying of Jesus: "for the tree is known by his _____"

142. What miracle did Jesus perform at the marriage in Cana?

143. What was the first thing Noah built when he came out of the ark?

144. Who claimed that the golden calf simply came out of the fire?

145. Towards which city was Saul travelling when he encountered a light from heaven?

146. What did the sailors of the ship Jonah was on do to increase their chances of survival?

147. Who was Jacob's mother?

148. How long will the Kingdom of God last?

149. Which is the longest Psalm?

150. In which town was Jesus born?

SECTION D

151. How were sins forgiven in the Old Testament?

152. How were the Thessalonians told to pray?

153. What happened to the city of Jericho after the priests blew their trumpets?

154. Which garden did Jesus go to, to pray in before his arrest?

155. Who was instructed by God to leave his home and family to travel to a country he did not know?

156. What was Jesus teaching about when he said, "What therefore God hath joined together, let not man put asunder"?

157. In the *Lord's Prayer*, what follows the line, "Hallowed be thy name"?

158. What was Jonah found doing on the ship while the storm was raging?

159. Five of the *Ten Virgins* did not take enough of what?

160. What was the name of Joseph's master in Egypt?

161. Aaron turned his rod into a serpent before Pharaoh, and Pharaoh's magicians did likewise, but what happened to their serpents?

162. To which country did Mary and Joseph escape when Herod killed all the babies in Bethlehem?

163. What is the name of the angel who appeared to Mary?

164. Which land did the Lord promise to Abram?

165. What should we "seek first"?

166. Which Psalm contains the line, "He leads me beside the still waters"?

167. In the parable of the ten virgins, what were they waiting for?

168. What event occurred to help release Paul and Silas from prison?

169. Which prisoner did the crowd call for to be released when Pilate asked them?

170. How does James say we should "treat the rich and the poor"?

171. How many plagues did God send on Egypt?

172. When Jesus asked "whom say ye that I am?" what did Peter reply?

173. What did King Solomon ask for when God appeared to him in a dream?

174. Who said, "Whosoever shall not receive the kingdom of God as a little child shall not enter therein"?

175. How did the angel of the Lord appear to Moses, when he was a shepherd?

176. Which of David's descendants will reign forever?

177. On what mountain did Moses receive the law from God?

178. Which of his wives did Jacob love the most?

179. What was the name of the ark where the commandments given to Moses were to be kept?

180. What did Jesus say to those who accused the adulteress?

181. Where is the "best place to pray"?

182. What does James say happens if we "draw nigh to God"?

183. Where was Jesus baptized?

184. Which plant is "the least of all seeds, but when it is grown, it is the greatest among herbs"?

185. Which city "came down from heaven prepared as a bride"?

186. At Capernaum, how did the man sick of the palsy gain access to the house in which Jesus was?

187. What did God breathe into Adam's nostrils?

188. What did Pharaoh's dream of good and bad ears of wheat represent?

189. To whom was the Revelation of Jesus Christ given?

190. How long was Jonah stuck inside the great fish for?

191. When Jesus walked on water, which sea was it?

192. Who told Joseph that Jesus would save his people from their sins?

193. Where did the man who received one talent from his master hide it?

194. To whom did Jesus say, "Why are ye fearful, O ye of little faith"?

195. What was the name of Hagar's son?

196. Who was Jacob's first wife?

197. What was Jesus wrapped in when he was born?

198. What did the Israelites do whilst Moses was receiving the Ten Commandments from God?

199. What guided the Israelites through the wilderness?

200. At what age did Jesus start his ministry?

Answers on Page 30

SECTION E

201. What animal spoke to Balaam?
202. What is the last book of the Old Testament?
203. What happened to Daniel after he gave thanks to God by his open window?
204. What was Jonah's reaction to the way the people of the city of Nineveh responded to God's message?
205. Zacharias and Elizabeth were told by an angel that they would have a son. What was he to be called?
206. How did Jesus say we should receive the Kingdom of God?
207. What happened to anyone who was not found written in the book of life?
208. In his Sermon on the Mount, what does Jesus say about tomorrow?
209. What did Joseph instruct to be put in Benjamin's sack?
210. What did Paul do to the soothsayer which made her masters unhappy?
211. What was the name of the place where Jesus Christ was crucified?
212. What object featured in Jacob's dream at Bethel?
213. What are the names of Joseph's parents?
214. What animal did Samson kill on his way to Timnah?
215. What was the name of Ruth's second husband?
216. Complete this common phrase of thanksgiving found in the Bible: "O give thanks unto the Lord; for he is good: for his _____ endureth for ever."

217. Who wrote the majority of the Psalms?
218. Which prophet anointed David as king?
219. A "soft answer turneth away..." what?
220. What job did the Prodigal Son end up taking after he had spent his inheritance?
221. Why shouldn't we give anyone the title of "Father"?

222. What kind of water does Jesus discuss with the Samaritan woman at the well?
223. How did Jesus heal the blind man?
224. Where did Jesus find Zacchaeus, the tax collector?
225. What is the name of Jesus' cousin, born six months before him?
226. Who was the first child born?
227. Which apostle, who was described as "full of grace and power, and doing great wonders and signs among the people", was stoned to death?
228. Who deceived Jacob by giving Leah as a wife instead of Rachel?
229. What did Jesus send disciples to fetch on his triumphal entry into Jerusalem?
230. In the parable of the lost sheep, how many sheep did the shepherd count safely into the fold?
231. What does James say we should say when we make our future plans?
232. What type of coin did Judas accept as payment for betraying Jesus?
233. What was the writer of the letter asking of Philemon?
234. What was the covenant between God and Noah?
235. Which prophet said, "Behold, a virgin shall be with child, and shall bring forth a son"?
236. To what object does James compare the tongue?
237. Which of David's sons rebelled against him?
238. What does Paul say about women's long hair?
239. What did Naomi tell the people in Bethlehem to call her?
240. When Jesus told his disciples to beware of the "leaven of the Pharisees and Sadducees", to what was he referring?
241. How was Daniel protected from the lions in the den?
242. "Everyone that is proud in heart" is what to the Lord?
243. What did John the Baptist say when he saw Jesus?
244. How did the city that Jonah was sent to react to God's message of destruction?
245. Who asked Jesus to remember him when he came into his kingdom?
246. Of what, specifically, was man not allowed to eat in the Garden of Eden?
247. What was Solomon famous for building?
248. Jesus asked: "Can the blind lead the....?"
249. Who told Peter to "watch and pray that he entered not into temptation"?
250. What is Paul's command to husbands in his letter to the Colossians?

SECTION F

251. Which river was Naaman told to wash in to rid himself of leprosy?

252. What miracle had Jesus performed when he said, "It is I; be not afraid"?

253. Why did Solomon turn away from God when he was old?

254. What is the "chorus" in Psalm 136 which is repeated in every verse?

255. In what city was Jesus brought up as a child?

256. Which female judge described herself as "a mother in Israel"?

257. After the angels had announced the birth of Christ and left the shepherds, what did the shepherds do?

258. According to Peter, what "covers a multitude of sins"?

259. In prison, for whom did Joseph interpret dreams?

260. To what preservative does the Lord compare his disciples?

261. What was Jesus' first miracle?

262. Who spotted Moses in the Nile placed in an ark of bulrushes?

263. Who was Bathsheba's first husband?

264. Why were Daniel's three friends thrown into the fiery furnace?

265. Out of the ten lepers who Jesus healed, how many came back to say thank you?

266. What did Jesus say the sellers had turned his house of prayer into?

267. In the New Jerusalem where are the names of the twelve tribes written?

268. How often was the year of the Lord's release?

269. Which tribe of Israel looked after the religious aspects of life?

270. Where was Paul when he wrote the letter to Philemon?

271. Who preached, "Repent ye: for the kingdom of heaven is at hand"?

272. What was the name of James' and John's father?

273. What bird did God provide to the Israelites for meat in the wilderness?

274. Who closed the door of Noah's ark?

275. "Hate stirs up strife", but what does love cover?

276. Who wrote the line: "The Lord is my Shepherd, I shall not want"?

277. Which prisoners experienced an earthquake after their prayer?

278. What was the name of Joseph's youngest brother?

279. Who did Jesus pray for that his faith failed not?

280. What was the new name given to Daniel while in captivity?

281. Which wise man wrote the majority of Proverbs?

282. Which king asked for the foreskins of 100 Philistines?

283. Who rolled away the tomb stone?

284. What did Samson find in the carcass of the animal he had killed at a later time?

285. What is "friendship with the world", according to James?

286. Who said "glory to God in the highest, and on earth peace, goodwill to men"?

287. In which book of the Bible does the story of Noah's ark appear?

288. When Samuel was called by the Lord as a child, who did he think was calling?

289. To whom did Jesus say "Truly, truly, I say to you, unless one is born again he cannot see the kingdom of God"?

290. Who does Paul say is head of the woman?

291. Who sang a song celebrating the downfall of Sisera?

292. What happens to "treasure laid up on earth"?

293. Whose mother was instructed to drink no wine or strong drink during her pregnancy?

294. Who was the successor to Moses?

295. What should you not "throw before swine"?

296. What was the name of the woman who hid the spies at Jericho?

297. In the letter to the Corinthians, who does Paul say is a "new creature"?

298. Which prophet is recorded as having an earnest prayer for no rain answered?

299. According to Thessalonians, what will happen to the believers alive at the return of Christ?

300. How did the Philistines discover the answer to Samson's riddle?

SECTION G

301. When he was approached by Jesus, who said, "What have you to do with me, Jesus, Son of the Most High God? I adjure you by God, do not torment me."?

302. What was the reason that Jacob and his family began a new life in Egypt?

303. How was Isaac's wife chosen?

304. Whose father was so pleased to see him that he gave him the best robe and killed the fatted calf?

305. What was the name of Solomon's son who succeeded him as king?

306. How did the people listening to the Sermon on the Mount view Jesus' teachings?

307. What does faith require to make it a living faith?

308. What did Jesus say you should do if someone asks you to go with them for a mile?

309. In the parable of the grain of mustard seed, when it becomes a tree birds come and do what?

310. The field that Judas Iscariot purchased with his betrayal money was called Aceldama, but as what was it also known?

311. Who did Jesus raise from the dead by a prayer of thanks to God?

312. The king's wrath is as "the roaring" of what?

313. What was the name of Ruth's son?

314. According to James, what happens if you break one commandment of the law?

315. "Go to the _____, thou sluggard; consider her ways, and be wise." What animal should we take lessons from?

316. How did the wise men know that the King of the Jews had been born?

317. What test did Elijah set the prophets of Baal, which failed, proving their god to be false?

318. Who was the tax collector that climbed up a tree so he could see Jesus?

319. What is Jesus' final commission to his disciples?

320. The Lord said that Jacob and Esau were two *what* in the womb?

321. When a man said to Jesus, "who is my neighbor?" what parable did Jesus reply with?

322. What happens to the man who "puts his hand to the plough and looks back"?

323. What did Samson do to the Philistines' crops after discovering his bride had been given to someone else?

324. Who was Jesus talking to when he taught the *Lord's Prayer*?

325. Ananias and Sapphira sold some property and secretly kept part of the proceeds for themselves. What happened to them?

326. To the beauty of which plant did Jesus compare to King Solomon?

327. What was on top of the Ark of the Covenant?

328. Who came to see Jesus by night?

329. For how long was the dragon bound in the bottomless pit?

330. Complete the Beatitude: "Blessed are the pure in heart..."

331. For how many pieces of silver did Judas betray Christ?

332. Who did Abram marry?

333. What did Jesus say he would leave with the disciples?

334. What did Paul ask Philemon to have ready for him?

335. In Egypt, what did Joseph accuse his brothers of at their first meeting?

336. Where did Jesus first see Nathanael?

337. Which disciple was a tax collector?

338. Which city was the letter to Philemon written from?

339. What horrific act did the women do to their children during the Babylonian siege of Jerusalem?

340. What does the name Abraham mean?

341. When the Pharisees asked Jesus whether it was lawful to pay taxes to Caesar, what object did he use to answer their question?

342. When Philip and the Ethiopian eunuch arrive at some water, what does the eunuch say?

343. Who said to Mary, "Blessed are you among women, and blessed is the fruit of your womb!"?

344. Seven fat and seven thin of what type of animal appeared to Pharaoh in a dream?

345. How old was Sarah when her son Isaac was born?

346. About what age was Jesus when he was baptized?

347. Which book comes after the book of Job?

348. How many horsemen are there in Revelation chapter 6?

349. What was the first temptation of Christ?

350. After the first king of Israel failed God, what was the name of the second man who was anointed king?

SECTION H

351. What type of tree did Zacchaeus climb to see Jesus?

352. When Jesus forgave the sins of the sick man let down through the roof to him, to what did the Pharisees object?

353. What was the name of Abraham's nephew?

354. Israel split into two kingdoms after the reign of King Solomon, with Israel in the north, but what was the name of the southern kingdom?

355. What did James' and John's mother ask of Jesus?

356. What did the dove bring back to Noah?

357. How many books are there in the New Testament?

358. Who was appointed to replace Judas Iscariot as a disciple?

359. What did Abraham's son carry for his sacrifice?

360. In which book of the Bible would we find Haman, the son of Hammedatha?

361. What did Elisha do for the Shunammite's son?

362. Which book of the Bible precedes Philemon?

363. What were the names of Elimelech's two sons?

364. Until when did Jesus remain in Egypt with his parents, when he was a baby?

365. In the parable of the sower, what does the seed represent?

366. What was the first plague the Lord sent upon Egypt?

367. What did the disciples do when people brought their young children to Jesus?

368. Who does Jesus say are the two most important people to love?

369. What happened to Jesus on the 8th day of his life?

370. Who looked after the coats of the men who stoned Stephen?

371. What profession did Zebedee, father of James and John, have?

372. Which two sisters married Jacob?

373. Into which land did God send Abraham to sacrifice his special son, Isaac?

374. In Revelation, what was the wife of the Lamb arrayed in?

375. Which Israelite woman had two Moabite daughters-in-law?

376. When Peter was asked if Jesus paid temple taxes, what animal concealed a coin with which to pay the taxes?

377. In Nebuchadnezzar's dream what did the different metals of the statue represent?

378. What did God initially give man to eat?

379. Which city did David pray for the peace of?

380. What did the crew of the ship Jonah was on do once the storm had ceased?

381. How many people were saved in the ark?

382. What disease did the Lord send upon Miriam?

383. The name of the Lord is like what place of safety?

384. With what was Jesus' side pierced?

385. Who wrote the book of Acts?

386. What did Jesus say when the Pharisees asked why he ate with publicans and sinners?

387. How did Moses command the Red Sea to divide so the Israelites could cross over?

388. Where was Jonah when he prayed to God with the voice of thanksgiving?

389. What was Noah's ark made out of?

390. Who brought Elijah bread and meat to eat during the drought?

391. Whose mother-in-law did Jesus heal?

392. Which bird does Jesus say we have more value than?

393. In which city was David's throne over Israel?

394. How old was Moses when he died?

395. What event did Peter, James and John witness in a mountain with Jesus?

396. Which apostle was a Pharisee?

397. The desolation of which city is described in Revelation chapter 18?

398. Which king in the Old Testament built the first temple in Jerusalem?

399. Why did Jesus say we should not "judge people"?

400. What happened to the prison keeper and his family after finding Paul and Silas released from their chains?

SECTION I

401. How is man "tempted"?
402. What natural disaster happened when Abram and Sarai arrived in the land of Canaan?
403. Which disciple did Paul commend for having "the same faith his mother had"?
404. What did the shepherds do after they had visited Jesus?
405. Who went back to Jerusalem after the captivity to encourage the people to build the walls of the city again?
406. Who was the first of the apostles to perform a miracle in the name of Jesus?
407. How did Korah and his family die after seeking priesthood duties beyond those they already had?
408. What was the name of Isaac's wife?
409. How does the Bible describe the location of the Garden of Eden?
410. In the vision of Jesus in Revelation, what came out of Jesus' mouth?
411. What was Paul's home town?
412. Which judge was betrayed to the Philistines by a woman?
413. What happened to forty-two of the children who made fun of Elisha's baldness?
414. What came out of the fire Paul made on Malta and attacked him?
415. Who refused to worship Nebuchadnezzar's golden image?
416. In the Sermon on the Mount, what did Jesus say would happen to the meek?
417. Where did Moses first meet his future wife?
418. Out of the ten lepers Jesus healed, what nationality was the one who returned to thank him?
419. Who did the men of Athens ignorantly worship?
420. What did Saul see on the road approaching Damascus?
421. How long did Jonah say it would be before Nineveh was to be overthrown?
422. What was the name of Samson's father?
423. Who did Amnon love, and then hate even more than he had loved her?
424. Where were the Jews taken captive to when Jerusalem was destroyed?
425. When was the festival of Passover established?
426. What sin did Noah commit after he began to be a "man of the soil"?
427. Why were the Israelites afraid to enter the Promised Land?

428. What did the silversmith do with Micah's silver?
429. What was Paul's profession?
430. What was the name of Ahasuerus' new queen?
431. According to the words of Jesus in the Sermon on the Mount, "a city that is on a hill cannot be..." *what*?
432. What was the fate of Shechem, the prince who fell in love with Dinah, daughter of Jacob?
433. What book of the Bible follows Philemon?
434. During Jacob's struggle with the angel, the hollow of which part of Jacob's body was touched and put out of joint?

435. Which Christian doctrine did the Sadducees reject?
436. For how many years had the woman with the issue of blood suffered before she was healed by Jesus?
437. What was the affliction of Bartimaeus?
438. What was the color of the robe placed on Jesus by the soldiers?
439. How did Paul say we should let our requests be made known to God?
440. In the Sermon on the Mount, what does Jesus tell us the earth is?
441. In which book of the Bible do we find "Nebuchadnezzar's image"?
442. Where was Abraham born?
443. Who was given a son following her prayer to God in the temple, during which the priest accused her of being drunk?
444. Who asked for an understanding heart to judge God's people?
445. What is "sin"?
446. For how long did David reign?
447. How many Psalms are there in the Bible?
448. Jesus used a little child to show the futility of an argument among the disciples. What were they arguing about?
449. Whose twelve year old daughter did Jesus raise from the dead?
450. What was the name of Ruth's great-grandson?

SECTION J

451. On what island was John when he was given the vision of Revelation?
452. What happened to King Nebuchadnezzar before being restored as king?
453. Where did Jonah try to run to instead of going to Nineveh as God had commanded?
454. Who did Paul send to Rome, requesting that she was given a welcome worthy of the saints?
455. Whose mother took him a little coat once a year?
456. Which judge killed Eglon, King of Moab?
457. In a parable told by Jesus, what did the rich man do with the surplus of crops that he grew?
458. In the parable of the leaven, what is leaven more commonly known as?
459. What bird could poor people use for sacrifices if they could not afford lambs?
460. Which book of prophecy was the Ethiopian eunuch reading from?
461. Who said, "When I was a child, I spake as a child, I understood as a child, I thought as a child: but when I became a man, I put away childish things"?
462. What is the first line of Psalm 1?
463. What was Peter's mother-in-law sick with?
464. Who instructed her daughter to ask for the head of John the Baptist?
465. Who decreed that a census of the entire Roman world should be taken at the time of Jesus' birth?
466. Which woman, who was "full of good works and acts of charity", was raised from the dead by Peter at Lydda?
467. What did Daniel do for Nebuchadnezzar that no-one else was able to do?
468. What was on the head of the woman "clothed with the sun"?
469. How did Uriah, Bathsheba's husband, die?
470. When Paul was shipwrecked on Malta how many people on the ship drowned?
471. How did Jesus say true worshippers should worship God when he was talking to the woman at the well?
472. Which profession does Jesus compare himself to spiritually?
473. Under the Mosaic Law, what was the punishment for someone who hit their father?

474. What presents did Pharaoh give to Joseph when he was given charge of Egypt?
475. What was taken off and handed over to signify the agreement between Boaz and the kinsman?
476. Peacocks were imported by which king of Israel?
477. Why did Boaz allow Ruth to glean in his field?
478. What punishment was Zacharias given for not believing the angel?
479. Which direction did the scorching wind upon Jonah come from?
480. Why did the kinsman not want to marry Ruth?
481. How many times did Samson lie about his source of strength to Delilah?
482. Which book of the Bible begins with "The book of the generation of Jesus Christ, the son of David, the son of Abraham."?
483. Jephthah made a vow to God, with what effect on his daughter?
484. Who did Mary suppose Jesus to be at first after the resurrection?
485. How did Jesus reveal the one who would betray him?
486. Which two Old Testament characters appeared with Jesus at the transfiguration?
487. Who prayed for the fiery serpents to be taken away from Israel?
488. Which married couple did Paul become friends with at Corinth?
489. Who persuaded Delilah to betray Samson?
490. When Jesus died, for how long was there darkness over the land?
491. What service did Nehemiah perform for King Artaxerxes?
492. What is the next line of the *Lord's Prayer* after "Give us this day our daily bread..."?
493. What did Abigail prevent David from doing to Nabal?
494. Who became nurse to Ruth's son?
495. According to the law, why could the Israelites not eat blood?
496. What relation was Jacob to Abraham?
497. What killed the plant that God had provided Jonah for shade?
498. What did the prophet Micah say about Jesus' birth?
499. What did John do with the little book he took from the angel?
500. Who went up yearly to worship God in Shiloh, and one year prayed to God for a baby?

SECTION K

501. In which tribe was the city of Bethlehem?

502. What was Peter doing when he denied Jesus for the second time?

503. What did Jonah do while he waited to see Nineveh's fate?

504. Who carried the cross for Christ?

505. On which mountain range did Noah's ark come to rest?

506. Which two tribes of Israel were not named after sons of Jacob?

507. What did the Queen of Sheba give to Solomon?

508. What should Philemon do if his slave owed him anything?

509. How many books are there in the Old Testament?

510. According to Old Testament law, what should you not cook a young goat in?

511. What did Joseph want to do when he discovered Mary was pregnant?

512. What did Boaz say Naomi was selling?

513. Abram was rich in gold, silver and what else?

514. How much of Elijah's spirit did Elisha receive?

515. What was unusual about the 700 Benjamite soldiers who could sling a stone and hit their target every time?

516. What relation was Annas to Caiaphas?

517. According to James, what is "pure and undefiled religion"?

518. When in prison at what time did Paul and Silas pray and sing to God?

519. What did Daniel and his three friends eat instead of the king's meat and drink?

520. What did Jesus say is the "greatest commandment in the law"?

521. Who was afflicted with leprosy for speaking out against Moses?

522. After the Babylonian exile, the Jews sought wealth and possessions for themselves. What should they have been doing?

523. What did God count Abram's faith to him as?

524. What sin stopped Moses from leading the children of Israel into the Promised Land?

525. Whose hair when cut annually weighed two hundred shekels by the king's weight?

526. During what traumatic event did the apostle Paul take bread and give thanks?

527. Which man killed a lion with his bare hands?

528. What was the sign that the angels gave to the shepherds, so that they would recognize Jesus?

529. Who was to be named Zacharias, after the name of his father, until his mother intervened?

530. In what town did Jesus turn water into wine?

531. How long had the infirm man lain at the pool of Bethesda?

532. What "doeth good like a medicine"?

533. What was God to give Abraham as an everlasting possession?

534. What lie was told about Naboth that led to him being stoned and Ahab taking possession of his vineyard?

535. Which supernatural being or beings does the Bible say the Sadducees did not believe in?

536. Who won the hand of Caleb's daughter, Achsah?

537. What is the "light of the body"?

538. The southern kingdom of divided Israel eventually fell, but to which great power?

539. You will be healed if you "pray for one another" and what else?

540. What is in the hypocrite's eye?

541. Which book of the Bible follows Jonah?

542. What inscription was on the altar in Athens?

543. In which book of prophecy do we read about the valley of dry bones?

544. Which baby was named after his mother's laughter?

545. Demetrius, of Ephesus was a...?

546. On which day of the year could the High Priest enter the Holiest Place, the inner most part of the temple where the covenant box was kept?

547. What was the name of the temple gate at which the lame man was laid daily?

548. To which Jewish sect did Nicodemus belong?

549. What is the first recorded dream of Joseph, son of Jacob?

550. To which tribe did the apostle Paul belong?

Answers on Page 34

SECTION L

551. How does James say we should "wait for the coming of the Lord"?

552. "The blessed man will be like a tree planted by".... *what*?

553. How old was Abraham when his son Isaac was born?

554. In the parable of the Pharisee and the Publican, what did the Pharisee thank God for?

555. How many times did Jesus say you should forgive your brother when he sins against you?

556. What question concerning marriage did the Pharisees use to tempt Jesus?

557. How does Paul tell us to "work out our own salvation"?

558. In the parable of the cloth and wine, why does no man put new wine into old bottles?

559. In which city did King Herod live at the time of Jesus' birth?

560. What is the "root of all evil"?

561. What does the law say to do when you see a bird in its nest?

562. Which tribe of Israel received no inheritance of land?

563. In Nebuchadnezzar's dream what happened to destroy the statue made from different metals?

564. Which King took possession of Naboth's vineyard?

565. For how many days did Jesus appear to his disciples after his resurrection?

566. Who did Paul write a letter to concerning his slave Onesimus?

567. How many churches of Asia Minor were listed in Revelation?

568. What object did Gideon place on the ground to receive a sign from God?

569. Why did Moses' hand become leprous?

570. In which city in Judah did Cyrus tell the Israelites to build the temple?

571. Which missionary was described as having "known the holy scriptures from an early age"?

572. What affliction did Paul strike Elymas the sorcerer down with?

573. Who was Boaz a kinsman of?

574. What animals were carved on Solomon's throne?

575. What did Jesus and the disciples have for breakfast when Jesus appeared to them after the resurrection by the Sea of Tiberias?

576. Which woman was a seller of purple goods?

577. What were the restrictions on marriage for the daughters of Zelophehad?

578. Who said, "A light to lighten the Gentiles, and the glory of thy people Israel," when he saw Jesus?

579. How did Moses assure victory against the Amalekites?

580. What was the occupation of Hosea's wife?

581. In the Sermon on the Mount, what does Jesus say you should do when you fast?

582. Which church did Jesus accuse of being lukewarm?

583. Why are the Thessalonians told not to worry about those Christians who have died?

584. In the parable of the sower, what happened to the seed that fell on the path?

585. What was the name of the man who requested Jesus' body for burial?

586. How many Philistines did Samson say he had killed with the jawbone of a donkey?

587. Which book of the Bible precedes Jonah?

588. Who did Samuel anoint as the first King of Israel?

589. What was mankind's first sin in the Bible?

590. What was the first bird released from the ark?

591. What nationality was Timothy's father?

592. In Revelation, what is the "number of a man"?

593. How many elders sat around the throne of God?

594. What order did Joshua give to God while fighting the Amorites?

595. How many years did the Lord add to Hezekiah's life after being healed of his sickness?

596. What was the second plague upon Egypt?

597. Which disciple looked after Mary, after the death of Jesus?

598. Jesus was a high priest after the order of which ancient king, mentioned in Psalm 110?

599. Which two provinces looked up to Thessalonica as an example?

600. Who was Noah's father?

SECTION M

601. Who did Pilate send Jesus to after he had interrogated him?

602. Daniel had a dream about four things. What sort of things?

603. In the parable of the sower, what did the seed that fell among thorns represent?

604. Who was the father of Jonah?

605. What relation to Abram was Lot?

606. Who will the "least person in the Kingdom of God" be greater than?

607. In what month of Elisabeth's pregnancy did the angel appear to Mary?

608. What was the content of the cupbearer's dream interpreted by Joseph?

609. "Hope deferred" maketh what sick?

610. Who laid their hands on Saul of Tarsus, curing him of the blindness he received on the road to Damascus?

611. Who was Paul with when he wrote the letter to Philemon?

612. What did Joseph send to his father from Egypt?

613. In which town did Martha and Mary live?

614. Who stole her father's household gods?

615. What was the fate of the man who had no wedding robe at the parable of the marriage feast?

616. How long did Solomon reign over Israel?

617. In Psalm 52, the psalmist describes himself as what kind of tree in the house of God?

618. Who was compared unfavorably to the lilies of the field?

619. Of what did Peter and John heal the man at the temple gate called Beautiful?

620. Which region was specially noted for its balm?

621. What should the Thessalonians do with brethren who are "not obeying the epistle's word"?

622. Why should a father not "provoke a child to anger"?

623. What did God rain down on the Amorite army as they passed through Beth-Horon, killing more of them than the Israelite army did?

624. While John was baptizing, what did he call the Pharisees and Sadducees?

625. Whose son did Elijah raise from the dead?

626. Which group of people stood and watched Jesus as he ascended into heaven?

627. What object did Elisha cause to float?

628. By what name was the disciple Tabitha also known?

629. From which land did Isaac tell Jacob not to take a wife?

630. How does Paul describe marriage in Hebrews?

631. To whom was Jesus referring when he said, "Go tell that fox, behold I cast out devils?"

632. How old was Joseph when he began serving Pharaoh?

633. What did Naboth refuse to sell?

634. Which living creatures in the water were deemed unclean?

635. What must a Christian do to "earn their own bread to eat"?

636. What was the name of the father of Caleb the spy?

637. Which apostle baptized the Ethiopian eunuch?

638. Who promised the "gift of power to tread on serpents and scorpions"?

639. Which king was saved from death by Abraham's prayer?

640. What did Abram do when he heard that Lot was made a prisoner of war?

641. Who sang, "My soul doth magnify the Lord"?

642. At what place did the Israelites arrive only to find the water was too bitter to drink, whereupon God caused it to become sweet?

643. Which Psalm describes how well the Lord knows man, starting with the line, "O Lord, thou hast searched me, and known me"?

644. When Moses blessed the tribes before his death, to what animal did he compare Gad?

645. When Saul defeated the Amalekites he disobeyed God and took possessions from the land. What was the name of the king he also spared?

646. What was Paul's "distinguishing mark" in the letters he wrote?

647. Which king had a feast using the gold and silver vessels taken from the temple in Jerusalem?

648. "The fear of the Lord is the beginning of knowledge, but fools despise"... what?

649. How should a "merry person" behave, according to James?

650. What sacrifice did Mary and Joseph offer when the days of purification were complete after Jesus' birth?

Answers on Page 35

SECTION N

651. Who sat down under a tree and asked the Lord to take away his life?

652. What god did the Philistines offer sacrifices to?

653. Which judge unknowingly vowed his daughter to the Lord as a burnt offering?

654. God appeared to Jacob on the way to Egypt in a vision at Beer-sheba, but what did he tell him?

655. What did God tell the people not to eat after the flood?

656. What punishment was given to Gehazi for his greed?

657. How did Rahab let the invading Israelites identify her house?

658. Which angel told Daniel the meaning of his vision of the ram and the goat?

659. Which king helped Solomon with his building projects?

660. How many missionary journeys did Paul undertake before his journey to Rome?

661. What was Timothy advised to take to help with his illnesses?

662. What happened to the prophet from Judah who was led to disobey God when a prophet from Bethel lied to him saying he was allowed to come back and share a meal with him?

663. Who was the goddess of the Ephesians?

664. How many volunteer soldiers did Gideon have initially?

665. What will Jesus "drink new in the Kingdom of God"?

666. What objects did Gideon and his army use to defeat the Midianites?

667. Who had a slave named Onesimus?

668. In which province was Thessalonica located?

669. Which is the shortest Psalm?

670. How did the townspeople regard Ruth?

671. In Revelation, how many people from each tribe were "sealed"?

672. Who slept under a juniper tree after fleeing for his life?

673. Who thought that the gift of God could be purchased with money?

674. What is described as a "tree of life to them that lay hold upon her"?

675. What relation was John Mark to Barnabas?

676. Finish the proverb: "The rod and reproof give wisdom, but a child left to himself."..

677. Why wasn't David allowed to build God's house?

678. Which parts of his body did Peter ask Jesus to wash, after being told that unless Jesus washed his feet he would have no part with him?

679. What did the Holy Spirit look like when the disciples received it?

680. Which two of the eight signs, or miracles, recorded in John, are also recorded in other gospel records?

681. Who led the people of Israel into the Promised Land?

682. With what object did Jael kill Sisera?

683. "Praise ye him, all his angels: praise ye him, all his hosts", is followed by which line?

684. Which of Leah's sons brought her mandrakes?

685. It is "better to obtain wisdom" than what?

686. In which book of the Bible do we read of David and Goliath?

687. Many of the chief rulers privately believed in Jesus. Why did they not confess this belief publicly?

688. When Jesus left Nazareth and began his ministry in Capernaum, what message did he preach?

689. According to James, what should we do after "confessing our faults to one another"?

690. How old was Joshua when he died?

691. Who was the king of Judea at the time of Jesus' birth?

692. What seed did Manna look like?

693. Which disciple brought the boy with five loaves and two fishes to Jesus?

694. According to James, what should we do when we "fall into temptation"?

695. Whose "days are like grass," according to the Psalmist?

696. Which animal is associated with the first four of the seven seals?

697. Which kind of bird did Jesus say were "sold two for a farthing"?

698. Who was the father of Abraham?

699. How were the family warned that someone wanted to kill the baby Jesus?

700. How did the sailors discover Jonah was responsible for the storm?

SECTION O

701. What did the chief priest and Pharisees give Judas to enable him to help arrest Jesus?

702. How old was Josiah when he became king of Judah?

703. What was the name of Abigail's first husband?

704. Why did Jephthah flee to the land of Tob?

705. Where did the hypocrites "love to pray"?

706. Who did Paul heal at Lystra?

707. Which animal did the ten spies liken themselves to, when compared to the people of the land of Canaan?

708. After Pilate found no guilt in Christ, for what reason did the Jews say that Jesus should die?

709. In a parable told by Jesus, two men went up to the temple to pray, a Pharisee and who else?

710. Who were the first two disciples to be called?

711. How many sons did Gideon have?

712. On which day of the creation did God create trees and plants?

713. On which island did Paul preach on his first missionary journey?

714. Why did the Pharisees deride Jesus when he said, "You cannot serve God and Mammon"?

715. What was Samson's offer of reward if the Philistines could solve his riddle?

716. How many of Nineveh's inhabitants could not "discern their left hand from their right hand"?

717. What did the mighty angel throw into the sea that represented the throwing down of Babylon?

718. God calls us to a life of holiness, but according to Thessalonians what are we told we are doing if we ignore this advice?

719. How did Paul escape from Damascus?

720. According to the Book of Proverbs, what is "bound in the heart of a child"?

721. Which men murdered the Levite's concubine?

722. What happened when the third vial of wrath was poured on the earth?

723. On what type of stone were the twelve children of Israel to have their names engraved, as part of the High Priest's garments?

724. What sin did Achan commit?

725. Who was the father of Saul?

726. What four beasts did Daniel see in a vision?

727. Wisdom is "more precious" than which gems?

728. What did the Israelites borrow from their Egyptian neighbors?

729. Who came into Galilee preaching the Kingdom of God?

730. What did God create on the fifth day?

731. What Egyptian name did Pharaoh give to Joseph?

732. What did Jesus do before driving the money-changers out of the temple?

733. What reward did Jesus say the twelve apostles would get for forsaking everything and following him?

734. Who said, "Worthy is the lamb who was slain"?

735. Who gave water to the camels of Abraham's servant, in answer to his prayer?

736. In which gospel does Jesus state that he is the "Bread of Life?"

737. How many fish were caught in the miracle of the draught of fishes?

738. From which minor prophet is Jesus quoting when he says, "I am come to set the daughter against her mother"?

739. After seeing the destruction of Jericho and Ai, the inhabitants of which city pretended to be travelers from a far off land to make a covenant of peace with the Israelites?

740. In the parable of the Good Samaritan, who was the first man to pass by the wounded man?

741. What did Paul do when he couldn't bear to be away from the brethren at Thessalonica any longer?

742. What did James and John want to do to the unwelcoming Samaritan village?

743. Jesus said not to "swear by your head" because you cannot do what?

744. On the fourth day God made the Sun, Moon and what else?

745. In the New Jerusalem described in Revelation, what are the twelve gates made from?

746. Which Psalm is entitled "A Prayer of Moses"?

747. On what day of creation were dry land and seas created?

748. How many tribes was Jeroboam promised he would rule over?

749. Which brother did Joseph imprison while the others returned to Jacob?

750. How many spies did Moses send out to explore the land of Canaan?

Answers on Page 36

SECTION P

751. Which bird does Job say is "lacking in wisdom", due to the fact she leaves her eggs on the floor?

752. Whose mother found him a wife from Egypt?

753. Noah was a "preacher" of what?

754. Which of the twelve sons of Jacob had a name that means "praise"?

755. What is the message of the parable that Jesus told Simon the Pharisee?

756. How many men and women were in the temple to watch Samson entertain them?

757. Who escorted the slave with the letter to Philemon?

758. Who was Paul writing to when he wrote "I will receive you and will be a Father unto you and ye shall be my sons and daughters, saith the Lord Almighty"?

759. What was the name of the servant who had his ear cut off at the arrest of Jesus?

760. What did Samson carry to the top of the hill overlooking Hebron?

761. Whose house did Paul go to in Caesarea?

762. Who went to sleep during one of Paul's sermons and fell out of the window?

763. Which prophet of God told Naaman to wash in the river Jordan to cure his leprosy?

764. What occupation did Priscilla have?

765. One title of God is El Shaddai, which means what?

766. What is the seventh commandment?

767. How many cities of refuge were on the east side of Jordan?

768. What was the name of Joseph's (son of Jacob) first born son?

769. According to the Bible what sort of man was Noah?

770. How many tribes inherited land on the east of Jordan?

771. What relation was Lois to Timothy?

772. In the parable of the Good Samaritan, who was the second man to pass by the robbed man?

773. What was the name of the city where Lydia was converted?

774. Against which enemy did Jephthah lead Israel?

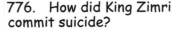

775. What was the name of the prophet who prophesied that Paul would be bound at Jerusalem?

776. How did King Zimri commit suicide?

777. In the parable of the laborers in the vineyard how much was each person paid to work?

778. Whose wife went into labor and gave birth on hearing the news that the Ark of God was captured and that her father-in-law and husband were dead?

779. In Luke's account of the Beatitudes who does Jesus say the Kingdom of God belongs to?

780. For what reason did Isaac say he loved Esau?

781. In the ritual cleansing of a leper under the Law of Moses, which animals were to be offered on the eighth day?

782. Who should you "withdraw from", according to the epistles of Thessalonians?

783. Psalm 91 verses 11 and 12 are quoted in which New Testament incident?

784. How was the earth watered initially before rain?

785. What proportion of his goods did Zacchaeus give away to the poor?

786. How old was Anna the prophetess when she saw Jesus?

787. What did Rachel steal from her father, Laban, when she left home with her husband Jacob?

788. The snail is mentioned in which Psalm?

789. How does Psalm 96 say we should worship God?

790. Why should children listen to "the instruction of a father"?

791. What did the disciples say to Jesus before the ascension?

792. What did Jesus eat to convince the disciples that he was indeed raised from the dead?

793. How old was Joseph when he died?

794. Where was David born?

795. How were the Thessalonians told to "keep their own bodies"?

796. How many companions did the Philistines give to Samson at the feast in Timnah?

797. How many times did Noah send out the dove?

798. What instruments were used to praise God when the temple foundation was rebuilt?

799. How many "minor prophets" are there?

800. "Honor thy father and thy mother" is one of the ten commandments. Which one?

SECTION Q

801. What did Daniel see by the river Hiddekel?
802. In the time of the Judges, civil war broke out against which tribe?
803. Paul thanks God that he did not baptize any of the Corinthians, except for which people?
804. Which Pharisee said that if the gospel truly comes from God, no-one will be able to stop it spreading?
805. Where does Solomon say that leopards live?
806. What did the New Jerusalem look like in the book of Revelation?
807. Melchizedek was a high priest, but also king of where?
808. Which king had the longest reign over the Kingdom of Israel?
809. On what day of the week was Christ resurrected?
810. Paul and Silas were imprisoned during the second missionary journey, but in what city did this happen?
811. What is the shortest book in the Old Testament?
812. In Matthew's account of the Sermon on the Mount, what was the first of the Beatitudes?
813. Jesus appeared to his disciples after the resurrection beside which sea?
814. How many wise men does the Bible say came to visit Jesus?
815. Where did Philip preach the good news about the Kingdom of God leading to many baptisms?
816. What did Paul do immediately after receiving his sight back?
817. What was the name of the city where Elijah raised the widow's son from the dead?
818. Who said, "To obey is better than sacrifice"?
819. What was the name of a man who was given the Spirit of God, to enable him to become a good craftsman, and assist with the building of the tabernacle?
820. Which prophet told Jeroboam he would rule over ten tribes?
821. What did Melchizedek give to Abram?
822. What argument prompted Jesus to tell his disciples that they would judge the twelve tribes in the kingdom?
823. Who was king of the southern kingdom when the northern kingdom of Israel fell to Assyria?
824. The fifth trumpet in Revelation is a plague which was also a plague upon Egypt in Exodus. Which one?
825. In Zechariah, the prophet has a vision of a man riding a red horse and standing under what kind of tree?
826. For how long did Abdon, son of Hillel, judge Israel?
827. When the Israelites came to Elim, how many palm trees were there?

828. How many rivers did the river in Eden split into once it left the garden?
829. What was the name of the Sorcerer Paul met on the island of Cyprus?
830. How much did Ruth glean on her first day in Boaz's field?

831. Who thanked King David for allowing his (David's) son Absalom to return to Jerusalem?
832. In the parable of the lamp, where is the candle to be "set once it is lit"?
833. "A wholesome (healing), tongue" is described as what?
834. Three of David's mighty men risked their lives against the Philistines to get him a drink of water from where?
835. What feast was instituted when Queen Esther saved the Jews from destruction?
836. What was the name of the field where Abraham buried his wife?
837. From which country did Solomon import horses?
838. What miracle did Jesus perform just before healing Legion of his unclean spirit?
839. Why did Pharaoh give Joseph's family the land of Goshen to live in?
840. After the exile, the Israelites returned and started to rebuild the temple in Jerusalem, but which other prophet along with Zechariah was sent to encourage the completion of the partly built temple?
841. At what place did the writer to the Thessalonians say he'd been given rough treatment?
842. Who was well reported of at Lystra and Iconium?
843. In John's first epistle which three things are said to testify and agree about Jesus?
844. In Proverbs, how shall the "man's belly be satisfied"?
845. What did Rahab hide the two spies under?
846. In years, roughly how long did Paul spend in Ephesus?
847. Which gospel records the fewest of the miracles performed by Jesus?
848. What does Psalm 16 say there is in "the Lord's right hand"?
849. Who walked barefoot and naked for three years at the Lord's command?
850. Who promised to give their daughters to Shechemites if they agreed to be circumcised, only to kill them instead three days later while they were still sore?

SECTION R

851. Which god did the people of Lystra think Paul was?

852. What happened to the sun when the sixth seal was opened?

853. What characteristics are attached to the breastplate mentioned in Thessalonians?

854. Of which animal were the kings of Israel told not to have lots?

855. In Revelation, unclean spirits came out of the mouth of the dragon, in the form of what animals?

856. How old was Noah when the floods came?

857. Which animal skins, dyed red, were used as an offering to help make the tabernacle?

858. Which king contributes words of wisdom in Proverbs chapter 31?

859. In which Jewish month is the Passover?

860. Who did Daniel see sitting in a throne in his vision of the four beasts?

861. The Ethiopian eunuch, held what office of responsibility to Candace, queen of the Ethiopians?

862. How does Psalm 100 say we should come before the Lord's presence?

863. How many concubines did Solomon have?

864. How did Moses make the bitter waters of Marah drinkable?

865. How did Adam and Eve feel about their nakedness at first?

866. Who deceived the worshippers of Baal into attending sacrifices only to destroy them all once they had arrived?

867. The branched candlestick in the tabernacle had its cups carved in the likeness of which plant?

868. What happened to the soldiers of Gideon who lapped the river water with their tongues like dogs?

869. How many sections (or books) is the book of Psalms split into?

870. How old was Abraham's first wife when she died?

871. To what does the "seventy weeks" prophecy refer?

872. To which tribe did Anna the prophetess belong?

873. What part of Paul's clothing did Agabus use?

874. David says in the Psalms that "adders' poison is under their lips". To whom is he referring?

875. Who was the father in law of Caiaphas, the high priest at the time of Jesus death?

876. Who did Paul take with him on his first missionary journey?

877. Jesus initially sent the twelve disciples to preach to which group of people?

878. Where will the believers reign in the Kingdom of God?

879. Who did Joseph's brothers sell him to?

880. Who shall the "prayer of faith" save?

881. Where did Delilah live?

882. Who was Paul referring to when he said, "May the Lord grant mercy to his household, for he often refreshed me and was not ashamed of my chains"?

883. How many elders witnessed Boaz's agreement with the kinsman?

884. According to Job, what is the hope of "a tree that is cut down"?

885. What should the Israelites not destroy when they besiege a city?

886. What offering did Gideon present to the Lord under the oak tree?

887. On what island was Paul shipwrecked as he made his way to Rome?

888. "An excellent wife" is a what to her husband?

889. To what tribe did Samson belong?

890. In which book of the Bible would you find the record of Balaam and his donkey?

891. What are Psalms 120-134 collectively known as?

892. When Joseph was in prison, whose dream did he correctly interpret to mean he would be restored to his job?

893. What is "sanctified by the word of God and prayer"?

894. In the parable of the good father, if a son asks for an egg, what would the good father not give him?

895. Fearing that Saul wanted to kill him, what lie did David ask Jonathan to tell his father if asked why he wasn't at the king's table for the New Moon feast?

896. What was the name of the field that Jacob requested to be buried in?

897. How long did Noah live for after the flood?

898. Paul, Timothy and who else sent their greetings to Thessalonica?

899. How many years did Jacob live for?

900. What animal is "better than a dead lion"?

SECTION S

901. One of the ten plagues of Egypt was the plague of boils, but which number was it?

902. After being left behind in Berea, in which city did Silas and Timothy meet up with Paul?

903. Who told his wife not to worry that she was barren and said, "am not I better to thee than ten sons"?

904. What does Job say is "poured out like water"?

905. A word "fitly spoken" is like what of gold set in pictures of silver?

906. On which occasion in the Bible does it specifically say that believers sung a hymn?

907. To which city did Samson go down to and kill thirty men?

908. Who was the Persian king when the rebuilding of the temple after the exile was finally complete?

909. What part of King Asa's body was diseased?

910. Which priest anointed Solomon?

911. Who does James say is the "source of every good and every perfect gift"?

912. Which disciple asked Jesus to show them the Father?

913. What did Athaliah do when she saw her son, Ahaziah, was dead?

914. Who had a bed 13.5 foot long by 6 foot wide?

915. Whose handkerchiefs were able to heal the sick?

916. How did Daniel react to the vision by the river Hiddekel?

917. Which Old Testament prophet was given a book to eat by God?

918. What was the name of the centurion who looked after Paul on the journey to Rome?

919. Which book of the Bible comments that "dead flies cause the ointment of the apothecary to send forth a stinking savor?"

920. "Bread gained by deceit is sweet to a man", but what shall his mouth be filled with afterwards?

921. What does Zechariah see in a vision that destroys the houses of thieves and liars?

922. How long did it take Solomon to build his own house?

923. At which battle were the Israelites defeated because Joshua attacked without seeking God's guidance first?

924. In the parable of the debtors, one owed 500 denarii (pence), but how much did the other one owe?

925. What was the name of the man who was paralyzed and had been bedridden for eight years?

926. How old was Abram when he first became a father?

927. How old was David when he died?

928. How long was Noah's ark?

929. During Paul's third missionary journey, roughly for how long did he minister in the school of Tyrannus at Ephesus?

930. What does James say "envying and strife in your heart" brings?

931. Which honorable counselor was waiting for the Kingdom of God?

932. One of the Ten Commandments forbids the coveting of a neighbor's property. Which one?

933. What did God specifically command concerning the eating of the thanksgiving offering that the Israelites made?

934. Which tribe's blessing from Jacob said they would "dwell at the haven of the sea"?

935. Jesus accused the Pharisees of hypocritically paying tithes on herbs, and omitting which weightier matters of the law?

936. Which king of Heshbon would not let the Israelites pass through his land?

937. What occasion did David write Psalm 105 for?

938. Which one of the Ten Commandments was an instruction not to lie (bear false witness)?

939. What was the name of the god that Barnabas was called at Lystra?

940. How many horns did the ram in Daniel's vision have?

941. Onesimus, was a run away slave from which city?

942. The disciple Thomas was also known as Didymus, but what does this name mean?

943. Which king decreed that the Jews could return to their land to rebuild the temple?

944. Isaiah took a cake of what to heal Hezekiah?

945. Who prayed, "I pray thee, open his eyes that he may see?"

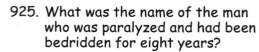

946. How many silver shekels did Jeremiah pay to Hanameel for a field in Anathoth?

947. In the love poetry of Song of Solomon the lady's hair is described as a flock of which animal?

948. What is the first offering made to the Lord recorded in the Bible?

949. In Revelation 22, who does it say has the right to the tree of life?

950. In Proverbs, what metal is the "tongue of the just" likened to?

Answers on Page 38

SECTION T

951. Which three tribes camped on the northern side of the tabernacle in the wilderness?

952. To where did Paul & Silas flee after upsetting the Jews at Thessalonica?

953. How many silver pieces would each Philistine lord give to Delilah if she betrayed Samson?

954. In the parable about a fig tree, when you see the "tree putting forth leaves", what is near?

955. According to Proverbs, how do those "seeking death" acquire their wealth?

956. In the prophecy of Isaiah, where will a little child play in the kingdom age?

957. In Genesis, who was buried under an oak tree below Bethel?

958. What color was the High Priest's robe?

959. Who does Paul thank God for because their "faith and love grew exceedingly"?

960. Which nation does Jeremiah say is dwelling in Gad?

961. In which city were Paul and Barnabas worshipped as gods?

962. What does the name Israel mean?

963. What must an Israelite do when "building a new house"?

964. Which prophet said, "Out of Egypt have I called my son"?

965. "Deceit is in the heart of them that"... do *what*?

966. Jesus quotes a portion of text from the Old Testament in connection with the parable of the vineyard owner, "The stone which the builders rejected is become the head of the corner:", but which Old Testament book did this come from?

967. Where did Paul leave the sick Trophimus?

968. In a battle against the Syrians, what killed 27,000 of them in the city of Aphek?

969. What weight of gold was Solomon recorded as acquiring in one year?

970. Who addresses an epistle to the "twelve tribes which are scattered abroad"?

971. Who was killed by a wet blanket?

972. In the parable of the Prodigal Son, what portion would the son have received?

973. What did Elisha throw into Jericho's water supply to "heal" it?

974. With what unusual weapon did Shamgar slay 600 Philistines?

975. In which tribe was the city of Ramoth-Gilead?

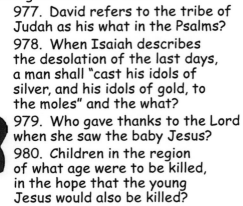

976. Why do the four and twenty elders in Revelation give thanks to God?

977. David refers to the tribe of Judah as his what in the Psalms?

978. When Isaiah describes the desolation of the last days, a man shall "cast his idols of silver, and his idols of gold, to the moles" and the what?

979. Who gave thanks to the Lord when she saw the baby Jesus?

980. Children in the region of what age were to be killed, in the hope that the young Jesus would also be killed?

981. Who is described in the Psalms as "spreading himself like a green bay tree"?

982. Aeneas was confined to bed for eight years suffering from the palsy, but which town did he dwell in?

983. Where was Solomon anointed?

984. Christ was led away to which high priest first?

985. Whose mother does Paul greet in the letter to the Romans?

986. Which Psalm does Paul quote from in his exhortation at Antioch?

987. "The legs of the lame hanging limp" are like what in the mouth of fools?

988. How does Peter say a husband should treat his wife?

989. After being told by God to remain in Gerar, who told the men there when questioned that his wife was merely his sister?

990. Why does David say "the daughters of Judah should be glad"?

991. For how many shekels of silver did Abraham purchase the field of Machpelah?

992. In Ezekiel's prophecy, who is said to be the "mother of Jerusalem"?

993. Who did Jesus say was "not far from the Kingdom of God"?

994. Who succeeded Herod the Great after his death?

995. On Paul's journey to Rome, at what location did he meet brethren whom he thanked God for?

996. Proverbs describes a "fair woman without discretion" as like a jewel of gold in what?

997. What does the name Abram mean?

998. How many begotten sons of David are named in the Bible?

999. In Luke's account of the Sermon on the Mount to who does Jesus say "God is kind"?

1000. How many cities did the Levites possess?

1001. The angel said to Mary that Jesus would "reign over the house" of which Old Testament character?

THE ANSWERS

The answers are generally taken from the KJV, but we have on occasions used other versions where appropriate. Answers will vary between different versions so we have provided the references and encourage you to look in your own Bible as the final authority. Occasionally we have provided references to Strong's Concordance of the Bible.

We have tried to make sure all the questions and answers are accurate but it is inevitable we have overlooked something (like an alternative answer we hadn't thought of).

If you do find an alternative answer, error or omission we would love to hear from you so we can amend the question or replace it in future editions and with your help we can make this book even better!

Please email info@biblequizzes.org.uk with your comments, providing Bible references where possible.

Answers - Section A

1. Mary (Matt 1:18)
2. Garden of Eden (Gen 2:8)
3. Loaves of bread and fishes (Matt 14:19)
4. Crucifixion (Mark 15:25)
5. Rib (Gen 2:21)
6. (Simon) Peter (Matt 26:69-74)
7. Serpent (Gen 3:1-6)
8. Crown of Thorns (Matt 27:29)
9. Our Father which art in heaven (Matt 6:9)
10. Daughter-in-law (Ruth 1:4)
11. Cain (Gen 4:9)
12. Abraham (Jam 2:21-22)
13. Creation (Gen 1 - 2)
14. King of the Jews / This is Jesus, King of the Jews (Mark 15:26; Matt 27:27)
15. Moses (Exo 2:3)
16. Forty (Gen 7:12)
17. She was a virgin (Matt 1:23)
18. Wise men / magi (Matt 2:7-10)
19. He was swallowed by a great fish (Jon 1:17)
20. God's (Gen 1:27)
21. Twelve (Luke 6:13)
22. Death (Rom 6:23)
23. Eve (Gen 4:1)
24. Shepherds (Luke 2:16)
25. Samson (Jdg 16:15)
26. Joseph (Matt 1:19)
27. Psalms (Ps 1:1-150:6)
28. Flood (Gen 7:7)
29. He ascended into heaven (Acts 1:3-11)
30. Pigs (Matt 8:32)
31. Two tables of stone (Deut 5:22)
32. Manger (Luke 2:7)
33. Dust of the ground (Gen 2:7)
34. Washed their feet (John 13:1-5)
35. Nineveh (Jon 1:2)
36. Jesse (Ruth 4:22)
37. John (Matt 1:1 - John 21:25)
38. Blasphemy against the Holy Spirit (Mark 3:29)
39. He hit him with a stone from his sling (1 Sam 17:49-50)
40. Threw him in a pit and then sold him to strangers (Gen 37:24-27)
41. Paul (Phm 1:1)
42. Linen clothes (John 19:40)
43. Aaron (Exo 7:1)
44. Murder (Gen 4:8)
45. Psalm 23 (Ps 23:1)
46. Revelation (Rev 1:1-22:21)
47. Paul (Rom 1:1 - Jude 1:25)
48. Shepherd (1 Sam 17:15)
49. Rahab (Josh 2:1-5)
50. Daniel (Dan 6:7)

Answers - Section B

51. Long hair (Jdg 16:17)
52. Egypt (Exo 13:3)
53. An angel (Dan 3:28)
54. Dipped his coat in the blood of a goat (Gen 37:31)
55. Fig (Gen 3:7)
56. The devil (John 8:44)
57. Tower of Babel (Gen 11:4,9)
58. The Lord's Prayer (Matt 6:9)
59. Abraham (Gen 17:5)
60. Rape (Gen 39:12-20)
61. Red Sea (Exo 13:18)
62. A rich man entering the Kingdom of God (Matt 19:24)
63. Forty (Josh 5:6)
64. Good fruit (Matt 7:17)
65. Tongue (Jam 3:5)
66. Sarah (Gen 17:15)
67. Rested (Gen 2:1-3)
68. Day of Pentecost (Acts 2:1-4)
69. Bread and wine (Matt 26:26-27)
70. Stones (Matt 4:3)
71. Pharisees and Sadducees (Mark 10:2)
72. Raised him from the dead (John 11:43-44)
73. Mt. Sinai (Exo 34:32)
74. David (1 Ki 2:12)
75. Carpenter (Matt 13:55)
76. With a kiss (Luke 22:48)
77. Threatened to divide the child (with a sword) (1 Ki 3:25)
78. Isaac (Gen 22:9)
79. In the temple (Luke 2:42-46)
80. A ghost (Matt 14:26)
81. John the Baptist's head (Matt 14:6-8)
82. Pushed the pillars over and the temple collapsed (Jdg 16:30)
83. Harp / Lyre (1 Sam 16:23)
84. Hunting (Gen 27:1-3,23)
85. To buy corn (Gen 42:2-3)
86. Jonathan (1 Sam 18:1)
87. Ruth (Ruth 1:16)
88. His (seamless) coat (Matt 27:35)
89. God with us (Matt 1:23)
90. Ask God for wisdom, in faith (Jam 1:5)
91. By a well (John 4:7)
92. (Simon) Peter (Matt 14:29)
93. Famine in his home town (Ruth 1:1-2)
94. Ananias & Sapphira (Acts 5:1-11)
95. Bathsheba (2 Sam 11:4)
96. Ring (Luke 15:22)
97. Sixty-six (Gen 1:1 - Rev 22:21)
98. Mary and Martha (John 11:1-3)
99. Nineveh (Jon 3:3)
100. A meal (Gen 25:30-34)

Answers - Section C

101. He died (Ruth 1:3)
102. Goes and looks for it (Matt 18:12)
103. Judas Iscariot (Mark 14:10)
104. Calf (Exo 32:4)
105. Mary Magdalene (Mark 16:9)
106. Fishermen (Matt 4:18)
107. Jonah (Jon 1:2-3)
108. Parables (Matt 13:10-13)
109. He was red and hairy (Gen 25:25)
110. Herod (the Great) (Matt 2:13)
111. Without form and empty (Gen 1:2)
112. He ran out and embraced him (Luke 15:20)
113. Psalm 23 (Ps 23:2)
114. Isaac (Gen 17:19)
115. Joseph (Gen 37:3)
116. Abraham (Matt 1:2)
117. Jerusalem (Zec 14:16)
118. Jesus (John 15:1)
119. God told him to strike a rock (Exo 17:6)
120. Judah (Heb 7:14)
121. An evil beast had devoured him (Gen 37:33)
122. She was barren (1 Sam 1:6)
123. The narrow gate (Matt 7:14)
124. His house fell flat (Matt 7:27)
125. Cousin (Luke 1:36)
126. Love your enemies, bless them
     that curse you (Matt 5:44)
127. God (Mark 1:11)
128. Benjamin (Gen 42:4)
129. Good news (Mark 1:1 / Strongs G2098)
130. Jonah himself (Jon 1:12)
131. Uncovered his feet and lay down
     next to him (Ruth 3:7)
132. Cunning hunter (Gen 25:27)
133. Washed and anointed his feet with
     precious ointment (Luke 7:36-46)
134. Washing herself (2 Sam 11:2)
135. Other gods (Exo 34:14; Deut 8:19)
136. Elijah (1 Ki 18:44-46)
137. Twelve (Gen 35:22)
138. Thomas (John 20:24-25)
139. Nebuchadnezzar (Dan 2)
140. Dove (Luke 3:22)
141. Fruit (Matt 12:33)
142. Water into wine (John 2:1-11)
143. Altar (Gen 8:20)
144. Aaron (Exo 32:24)
145. Damascus (Acts 9:3)
146. Threw the cargo overboard (Jon 1:5)
147. Rebekah (Gen 27:11)
148. Forever (2 Pe 1:11)
149. Psalm 119 (Ps 119)
150. Bethlehem (Matt 2:1)

Answers - Section D

151. Animal sacrifice (Lev 4)
152. Without ceasing (1 Th 5:17)
153. Walls fell down (Josh 6:20)
154. Gethsemane (Matt 26:36)
155. Abraham (Abram) (Gen 12:1)
156. Marriage (and divorce) (Matt 19:6)
157. Thy kingdom come (Matt 6:10)
158. Sleeping (Jon 1:5)
159. Oil (Matt 25:3)
160. Potiphar (Gen 37:36)
161. Aaron's rod swallowed them (Exo 7:12)
162. Egypt (Matt 2:13-14)
163. Gabriel (Luke 1:26)
164. Canaan (Gen 17:8)
165. The Kingdom of God and his
     righteousness (Matt 6:33)
166. Psalm 23 (Ps 23:2)
167. Bridegroom (Matt 25:1)
168. Earthquake (Acts 16:26)
169. Barabbas (Matt 27:21)
170. Do not judge them, but treat them
     impartially (Jam 2:1-4)
171. Ten (Exo 7:14-12:30)
172. Thou art the Christ, the Son of
     the Living God (Matt 16:16)
173. Wisdom (to judge between
     good and evil) (1 Ki 3:9)
174. Jesus (Luke 18:16-17)
175. From within a burning bush (Exo 3:2)
176. Jesus (Luke 1:32-33)
177. Mount Sinai (Lev 26:46)
178. Rachel (Gen 29:30)
179. Ark of the Covenant (Deut 10:2,8)
180. He that is without sin, let him first
     cast a stone (John 8:7)
181. In your closet with the door shut (Matt 6:6)
182. He will draw nigh to us (Jam 4:8)
183. River Jordan (Mark 1:9)
184. Mustard (Matt 13:31-32)
185. New Jerusalem (Rev 21:2)
186. Through the roof (Mark 2:4)
187. The breath of life (Gen 2:7)
188. Seven years of plenty followed by
     seven years of famine (Gen 41:29)
189. John (Rev 1:1)
190. Three days (Jon 1:17)
191. Sea of Galilee (John 6:1-19)
192. Angel of the Lord (Matt 1:21)
193. In the ground (Matt 25:25)
194. The disciples (Matt 8:26)
195. Ishmael (Gen 16:15)
196. Leah (Gen 29)
197. Swaddling clothes (Luke 2:7)
198. Made a golden calf (Deut 9:15-16)
199. A pillar of cloud and of fire (Exo 13:21)
200. Thirty (Luke 3:23)

Answers - Section E

201. Donkey (Num 22:28)
202. Malachi (Mal 4:6 - Matt 1:1)
203. He was thrown into the lions' den (Dan 6:10,16)
204. He was angry (Jon 4:1)
205. John (Luke 1:13)
206. As a little child (Luke 18:17)
207. They were cast in the lake of fire (Rev 20:15)
208. Take no thought for it (Matt 6:34)
209. His grain money and a silver cup (Gen 44:2)
210. Commanded the spirit of divination to leave her (Acts 16:18-19)
211. Golgotha / Calvary (John 19:17)
212. Ladder (Gen 28:12)
213. Jacob and Rachel (Gen 46:19)
214. Lion (Jdg 14:6)
215. Boaz (Ruth 4:13)
216. Mercy (Ps 106:1)
217. David (Ps 1 - 150)
218. Samuel (1 Sam 16:13)
219. Wrath (Pro 15:1)
220. Pig feeder (Luke 15:15)
221. We have one father, who is in heaven (Matt 23:9)
222. Living water (John 4:10)
223. He covered his eyes with clay and told him to wash (John 9:6-7)
224. Up a tree (Luke 19:4-5)
225. John (Luke 1:36)
226. Cain (Gen 4:1)
227. Stephen (Acts 7:59)
228. Laban (Gen 29:25)
229. Donkey and colt (Matt 21:1-2)
230. Ninety-nine (Matt 18:12)
231. If the Lord will, I will do this or that (Jam 4:15)
232. Silver (Matt 26:15)
233. To receive his slave back as a brother in Christ (Phm 1:17)
234. Never to flood the earth again (Gen 9:11)
235. Isaiah (Isa 7:14)
236. The rudder on a ship (Jam 3:4)
237. Absalom (2 Sam 15)
238. It is a glory to her (given as a covering) (1 Cor 11:15)
239. Mara (Ruth 1:20)
240. The doctrines of the Pharisees and Sadducees (Matt 16:12)
241. An angel shut their mouths (Dan 6:22)
242. An abomination (Pro 16:5)
243. Behold the Lamb of God! (John 1:29)
244. They repented (Jon 3:8)
245. The criminal on the cross (Luke 23:42)
246. Tree of knowledge of good and evil (Gen 2:17)
247. Temple (1 Ki 7:51)
248. Blind (Luke 6:39)
249. Jesus (Matt 26:40-41)
250. Love your wives, and do not be bitter towards them (Col 3:19)

Answers - Section F

251. Jordan (2 Ki 5:10)
252. Walking on water (John 6:19-20)
253. His foreign wives turned his heart after other gods (1 Ki 11:4)
254. For his mercy endureth forever (Ps 136)
255. Nazareth (Matt 2:23)
256. Deborah (Jdg 5:7)
257. Went quickly to Bethlehem (Luke 2:15-16)
258. Love (1 Pe 4:8)
259. The butler and the baker (Gen 40:5)
260. Salt (Matt 5:13)
261. Changing water into wine (John 2:11)
262. Pharaoh's daughter (Exo 2:5)
263. Uriah (2 Sam 11:3)
264. They wouldn't bow down to Nebuchadnezzar's golden image (Dan 3:11-12)
265. One (Luke 17:15)
266. A den of thieves (Luke 19:46)
267. On the twelve gates (Rev 21:12)
268. Every seven years (Deut 15:1-2)
269. Levi (Num 18:20-24)
270. In prison (Phm 1:23)
271. John the Baptist (Matt 3:1-2)
272. Zebedee (Mark 10:35)
273. Quail (Exo 16:13)
274. God (Gen 7:16)
275. All sins (Pro 10:12)
276. David (Ps 23:1)
277. Paul and Silas (Acts 16:26)
278. Benjamin (Gen 44:12)
279. (Simon) Peter (Luke 22:32)
280. Belteshazzar (Dan 1:7)
281. Solomon (Pro 1:1)
282. Saul (1 Sam 18:25)
283. An Angel (Matt 28:2)
284. Bees and honey (Jdg 14:8)
285. Enmity with God (Jam 4:4)
286. Angels (Luke 2:13-14)
287. Genesis (Gen 6 - 8)
288. Eli, the priest (1 Sam 3:2-6)
289. Nicodemus (John 3:3)
290. Man (1 Cor 11:3)
291. Deborah & Barak (Jdg 5:1)
292. Becomes corrupted and thieves steal it (Matt 6:19)
293. Samson's (Jdg 13:7)
294. Joshua (Josh 1:1-6)
295. Pearls (Matt 7:6)
296. Rahab (Josh 2:3-4)
297. Any man in Christ (2 Cor 5:17)
298. Elijah (Jam 5:17)
299. They will be caught up together in the clouds (1 Th 4:17)
300. They threatened Samson's bride, who told them (Jdg 14:15)

Answers - Section G

301. Legion (Mark 5:7)
302. Famine in Canaan (Gen 47:4)
303. His father sent a servant back to Mesopotamia to choose a wife from his own family (Gen 24)
304. Prodigal son (Luke 15:23-24)
305. Rehoboam (1 Ki 11:43)
306. He taught as one with authority (Matt 7:29)
307. Works (Jam 2:17)
308. Go with them for two miles (Matt 5:41)
309. Build nests (Matt 13:32)
310. Field of Blood (Acts 1:19)
311. Lazarus (John 11:41)
312. A lion (Pro 19:12)
313. Obed (Ruth 4:17)
314. You are guilty of breaking the whole law (Jam 2:10)
315. Ant (Pro 6:6)
316. They saw a star in the East (Matt 2:2)
317. Lighting a fire under the sacrifice on the altar (1 Ki 18:24)
318. Zacchaeus (Luke 19:5)
319. Teach all nations, baptizing them (Matt 28:19)
320. Nations (Gen 25:23)
321. The good Samaritan (Luke 10:29)
322. He is not fit for the Kingdom of God (Luke 9:62)
323. Burned them (Jdg 15:5)
324. Disciples (Matt 5:1)
325. They died (Acts 5:1-11)
326. Lilies (of the field) (Luke 12:27)
327. The mercy seat and two cherubim (Exo 25:22)
328. Nicodemus (John 19:39)
329. 1,000 years (Rev 20:1-3)
330. ...for they shall see God. (Matt 5:8)
331. Thirty (Matt 26:15)
332. Sarai (Gen 11:29)
333. Peace (John 14:27)
334. A room (Phm 1:22)
335. Being spies (Gen 42:9)
336. Under the fig tree (John 1:48)
337. Matthew (Levi) (Luke 5:27)
338. Rome (while under house arrest) (Phm 1:23)
339. Boiled and ate them (Lam 4:10)
340. Father of a multitude (Gen 17:5)
341. A penny (denarius) (Matt 22:19)
342. What is there to stop me getting baptized? (Acts 8:36)
343. Elisabeth (Luke 1:41-42)
344. Cattle (or Cows) (Gen 41:1-4)
345. Ninety (Gen 17:17; 21:5)
346. Thirty (Luke 3:23)
347. Psalms (Job 42:17 - Ps 1:1)
348. Four (Rev 6:2-8)
349. To turn a stone into bread (Matt 4:3)
350. David (1 Sam 16:1,13)

Answers - Section H

351. Sycamore (Luke 19:4)
352. They thought only God could forgive sins (Mark 2:7)
353. Lot (Gen 12:5)
354. Judah (1 Ki 11:31-36; 12:20-21)
355. For her sons to sit on Jesus' right and left hands in the kingdom (Matt 20:21)
356. Olive leaf (Gen 8:11)
357. Twenty-seven (Matt 1:1 - Rev 22:21)
358. Matthias (Acts 1:26)
359. The wood (Gen 22:6)
360. Esther (Est 3:1)
361. Raised him back to life (2 Ki 4:32-37)
362. Titus (Tit 3:15 - Phm 1:1)
363. Mahlon & Chilion (Ruth 1:2)
364. Until the death of Herod the Great (Matt 2:15)
365. Word of God (Luke 8:11)
366. Water turned into blood (Exo 7:21)
367. They rebuked them (Matt 19:13)
368. God and your neighbor (Luke 10:27)
369. He was circumcised (Luke 2:21)
370. Saul (Acts 7:58)
371. Fisherman (Matt 4:21)
372. Rachel and Leah (Gen 29:28)
373. Moriah (Gen 22:2)
374. Fine white linen (Rev 19:8)
375. Naomi (Ruth 1:4)
376. Fish (Matt 17:27)
377. Kingdoms of the world (Dan 2:37-44)
378. Plants and Fruit (Gen 2:9,16)
379. Jerusalem (Ps 122:6)
380. They made sacrifices to God (Jon 1:16)
381. Eight (1 Pe 3:20)
382. Leprosy (Num 12:10)
383. A strong tower (Pro 18:10)
384. Spear (John 19:34)
385. Luke (Acts 1:1 (cf Luke 1:3))
386. They that be whole need not a physician, but they that are sick. (Matt 9:11-12)
387. He lifted up his rod and stretched his hand over the sea (Exo 14:16,21)
388. In the fish's belly (Jon 2:9)
389. Gopher (cypress) wood (Gen 6:14)
390. Ravens (1 Ki 17:4)
391. (Simon) Peter's (Matt 8:14-15)
392. Sparrow (Matt 10:31)
393. Jerusalem (2 Sam 5:5)
394. 120 (Deut 34:7)
395. Transfiguration (Matt 17:1)
396. Paul (Acts 23:6)
397. Babylon (Rev 18:2)
398. Solomon (2 Chr 3:1)
399. So that we are not judged (Matt 7:1)
400. They believed and were baptized (Acts 16:33)

Answers – Section I

401. He is enticed by his own lust (Jam 1:14)
402. A famine (Gen 12:10)
403. Timothy (2 Tim 1:5)
404. Spread the news about Jesus' birth (Luke 2:17)
405. Nehemiah (Neh 2:17)
406. Peter (Acts 3:6)
407. They were swallowed up by the earth (Num 16:1-35)
408. Rebekah (Gen 24:67)
409. In the east (Gen 2:8)
410. A sharp sword (Rev 19:15)
411. Tarsus (Acts 21:39)
412. Samson (Jdg 16:5-6)
413. Two bears came out of the woods and killed them (2 Ki 2:24)
414. Viper (Acts 28:3)
415. Shadrach, Meshach and Abednego (Dan 3:12)
416. They will inherit the earth (Matt 5:5)
417. By a well in the land of Midian (Exo 2:16-21)
418. Samaritan (Luke 17:16)
419. The Unknown God (Acts 17:22-23)
420. A shining light from heaven (Acts 9:3)
421. Forty days (Jon 3:4)
422. Manoah (Jdg 13:24)
423. Tamar (2 Sam 13:15)
424. Babylon (Jer 29:4)
425. When the plague of the death of the firstborn was brought upon the land of Egypt (Exo 12:27)
426. Drunkenness (Gen 9:20-21)
427. The inhabitants were great and tall (Num 13:33-14:4)
428. Made it into an idol (Jdg 17:4)
429. Tentmaker (Acts 18:3)
430. Esther (Est 2:17)
431. Hidden (Matt 5:14)
432. He, his father, and the men of his city were slain by Dinah's brothers (Gen 34)
433. Hebrews (Phm 1:25 - Heb 1:1)
434. Hollow of thigh / Hip (Gen 32:25)
435. Resurrection (Matt 22:23)
436. Twelve years (Matt 9:20)
437. Blind (Mark 10:46)
438. Scarlet / Purple (Matt 27:28; John 19:2)
439. By prayer and supplication with thanksgiving (Php 4:6)
440. God's footstool (Matt 5:35)
441. Daniel (Dan 2:31-36)
442. Ur (Gen 11:31)
443. Hannah (1 Sam 1:13)
444. Solomon (1 Ki 3:9)
445. The transgression of the law (1 Jn 3:4)
446. Forty years (2 Sam 5:4)
447. 150 (Ps 1:1-150:6)
448. Who is the greatest in heaven (Matt 18:1-4)
449. Jairus' (Luke 8:41)
450. David (Ruth 4:22)

Answers – Section J

451. Patmos (Rev 1:9)
452. He went mad and lived as a beast (Dan 4:33-36)
453. Tarshish (Jon 1:3)
454. Phoebe (Rom 16:1-2)
455. Samuel (1 Sam 2:19)
456. Ehud (Jdg 3:15-25)
457. Built larger barns to store them (Luke 12:18)
458. Yeast (Matt 13:33)
459. Turtledoves or Pigeons (Lev 5:7)
460. Isaiah (Acts 8:30)
461. Paul (1 Cor 13:11)
462. Blessed is the man who walks not in the counsel of the ungodly (Ps 1:1)
463. A fever (Matt 8:14)
464. Herodias (Matt 14:8)
465. Augustus Caesar (Luke 2:1)
466. Tabitha (Dorcas) (Acts 9:40)
467. Interpret his dreams (Dan 2)
468. A crown of twelve stars (Rev 12:1)
469. Cut down after David instructed his men to abandon Uriah in battle (2 Sam 11:15)
470. None (Acts 27:22,44)
471. In spirit and truth (John 4:23-24)
472. Shepherd (John 10:14)
473. Death (Exo 21:15)
474. His ring, fine linen and a gold chain (Gen 41:42)
475. Sandal (Ruth 4:8)
476. Solomon (1 Ki 10:22)
477. She had looked after Naomi (Ruth 2:11)
478. He was made dumb (Luke 1:20)
479. East (Jon 4:8)
480. Didn't want to spoil his inheritance (Ruth 4:6)
481. Three (Jdg 16:15)
482. Matthew (Matt 1:1)
483. Her life was sacrificed to God (Jdg 11:30-40)
484. Gardener (John 20:15)
485. Dipped a piece of bread and passed it to him (John 13:26)
486. Elijah and Moses (Matt 17:3)
487. Moses (Num 21:7)
488. Aquila and Priscilla (Acts 18:2)
489. Lords of the Philistines (Jdg 16:5)
490. Three hours (Luke 23:44)
491. Cupbearer (Neh 1:11)
492. And forgive us our debts/ sins (Matt 6:11-12; Luke 11:4)
493. Murdering him (1 Sam 25:34-35)
494. Naomi (Ruth 4:16)
495. God said, "the blood is the life." (Deut 12:23)
496. Grandson (Matt 1:2)
497. A worm (Jon 4:7)
498. He would be born in Bethlehem (Mic 5:2)
499. He ate it (Rev 10:10)
500. Hannah (1 Sam 1:3-11)

501. Judah (Mic 5:2)
502. Warming himself by a fire (John 18:25)
503. He sat down on the East of the city and made a shelter (Jon 4:5)
504. Simon of Cyrene (Matt 27:32)
505. Ararat (Gen 8:4)
506. Ephraim and Manasseh (Josh 14:4)
507. (120 talents of) gold, spices, and precious stones (1 Ki 10:10)
508. Charge it to Paul (Phm 1:18)
509. Thirty-nine (Gen 1:1 - Mal 4:6)
510. Its mother's milk (Ex 23:19)
511. (Quietly) divorce her (Matt 1:19)
512. A parcel of land (Ruth 4:3)
513. Cattle (Gen 13:2)
514. Double (portion) (2 Ki 2:9)
515. They were all left-handed (Jdg 20:16)
516. Father-in-law (John 18:13)
517. To visit the fatherless and widows, and to keep yourself unspotted from the world (Jam 1:27)
518. Midnight (Acts 16:25)
519. Pulses and water (Dan 1:12)
520. To love God with all your heart, soul and mind (Mark 12:29-30)
521. Miriam (Num 12:10)
522. Rebuilding the temple (Hag 1:2-6)
523. Righteousness (Gen 15:6)
524. Hitting a rock twice (instead of speaking to it) (Num 20:11)
525. Absalom (2 Sam 14:26)
526. Sea voyage (Acts 27:35)
527. Samson (Jdg 14:5-6)
528. Wrapped in swaddling clothes, lying in a manger (Luke 2:12)
529. John (Luke 1:60)
530. Cana (John 2:1-11)
531. Thirty-eight years (John 5:5)
532. A merry heart (Pro 17:22)
533. The land of Canaan (Gen 17:8)
534. He had blasphemed against God and the king (1 Ki 21:10)
535. Angels (Acts 23:8)
536. Othniel (Josh 15:16-17)
537. The eye (Matt 6:22)
538. Babylon (2 Ki 25)
539. Confess your faults (Jam 5:16)
540. A beam (Matt 7:5)
541. Micah (Jon 4:11 - Mic 1:1)
542. To the Unknown God (Acts 17:23)
543. Ezekiel (Eze 37:1)
544. Isaac (Gen 21:6 / Strong's H3327)
545. Silversmith (Acts 19:24)
546. Day of Atonement (Lev 16)
547. Beautiful Gate (Acts 3:2)
548. Pharisees (John 3:1)
549. Sheaves of wheat bowing down to other sheaves (Gen 37:5-7)
550. Benjamin (Rom 11:1)

551. Patiently (Jam 5:7)
552. Rivers of water (Ps 1:1-3)
553. 100 (Gen 21:5)
554. That he was not sinful like other men (Luke 18:11)
555. Seventy times seven (Matt 18:22)
556. Is it lawful for a man to put away his wife? (Divorce) (Matt 19:3)
557. With fear and trembling (Php 2:12)
558. It will burst the bottles (Luke 5:37)
559. Jerusalem (Matt 2:3)
560. Love of money (1 Tim 6:10)
561. Let the mother bird go free (Deut 22:6-7)
562. Levi (Deut 10:9)
563. A stone hit the feet and broke them into pieces (Dan 2:34)
564. Ahab (1 Ki 21:16)
565. Forty (Acts 1:3)
566. Philemon (Phm 1:1-25)
567. Seven (Rev 1:11)
568. Fleece (Jdg 6:37)
569. As a sign (Exo 4:6-8)
570. Jerusalem (Ezr 6:3)
571. Timothy (2 Tim 3:15)
572. Blindness (Acts 13:8,11)
573. Elimelech (Ruth 2:1)
574. Lions (1 Ki 10:19)
575. Bread and fish (John 21:13)
576. Lydia (Acts 16:14)
577. They must marry within their tribe (Num 36:6)
578. Simeon (Luke 2:25,32)
579. Kept his hands held up (Exo 17:11-12)
580. Harlot (Hos 1:2)
581. Anoint your head, and wash your face (Matt 6:18)
582. Laodicea (Rev 3:16)
583. They will be raised to life again (1 Th 4:13-15)
584. Eaten by birds (Matt 13:4)
585. Joseph (of Arimathaea) (Matt 27:57-58)
586. 1,000 (Jdg 15:16)
587. Obadiah (Oba 1:21 - Jon 1:1)
588. Saul (1 Sam 10:1,19-24)
589. Eating some fruit (Gen 3:6)
590. Raven (Gen 8:7)
591. Greek (Acts 16:1)
592. 666 (Rev 13:18)
593. Twenty-four (Rev 4:4)
594. Make the sun and moon stand still (Josh 10:12-14)
595. Fifteen (2 Ki 20:6)
596. Frogs (Exo 8:6)
597. John (John 19:26-27)
598. Melchizedek (Ps 110:4)
599. Macedonia & Achaia (1 Th 1:7)
600. Lamech (Gen 5:28-29)

Answers - Section M

601. Herod (Luke 23:7)
602. Beasts (Dan 7:3)
603. Those people who hear God's word but then it's choked out by worldly cares (Matt 13:22)
604. Amittai (Jon 1:1)
605. His nephew (Gen 14:12)
606. John the Baptist (Luke 7:28)
607. Sixth (Luke 1:26)
608. A vine bringing forth grapes which are pressed into a cup (Gen 40:9-12)
609. The heart (Pro 13:12)
610. Ananias (Acts 9:17)
611. Timothy (Phm 1:1)
612. Ten male donkeys and ten female donkeys laden with goods from Egypt (Gen 45:23)
613. Bethany (John 11:1)
614. Rachel (Gen 31:32)
615. Cast into darkness (Matt 22:13)
616. Forty years (1 Ki 11:42)
617. Olive (Ps 52:8)
618. King Solomon (Matt 6:28-29)
619. Lameness (Acts 3:2)
620. Gilead (Jer 46:11)
621. Have no company with them so that they are ashamed (2 Th 3:14)
622. In case they become discouraged (Col 3:21)
623. Hailstones (Josh 10:11)
624. Generation of vipers (Matt 3:7)
625. The widow of Zarephath (1 Ki 17:22)
626. Men of Galilee (Disciples) (Acts 1:11)
627. Axe head (2 Ki 6:5-6)
628. Dorcas (Acts 9:36)
629. Canaan (Gen 28:1)
630. Honorable (Heb 13:4)
631. Herod (Luke 13:31-32)
632. Thirty (Gen 41:46)
633. Vineyard (1 Ki 21:2-3)
634. Those without fins and scales (Deut 14:9)
635. Work quietly (2 Th 3:12)
636. Jephunneh (Num 13:6)
637. Philip (Acts 8:38)
638. Jesus (Luke 10:19)
639. Abimelech (Gen 20:17)
640. Fought to rescue him (Gen 14:14-16)
641. Mary (Luke 1:46)
642. Marah (Exo 15:23)
643. Psalm 139 (Ps 139:1)
644. Lion (Deut 33:20)
645. Agag (1 Sam 15:9)
646. He wrote the greetings in his own handwriting (2 Th 3:17)
647. Belshazzar (Dan 5:2)
648. Wisdom and instruction (Pro 1:7)
649. Sing psalms (Jam 5:13)
650. Two turtledoves or pigeons (Luke 2:24)

Answers - Section N

651. Elijah (1 Ki 19:4)
652. Dagon (Jdg 16:23)
653. Jephthah (Jdg 11:30-40)
654. Don't fear going to Egypt, he would be made into a great nation there (Gen 46:3)
655. Blood (Gen 9:4)
656. Made leprous (2 Ki 5:25-27)
657. She tied a red thread in the window (Josh 2:18)
658. Gabriel (Dan 8:16)
659. Hiram, King of Tyre (1 Ki 7:13)
660. Three (Acts 13 - 21)
661. Wine (1 Tim 5:23)
662. Killed by a lion (1 Ki 13:24)
663. Diana (Artemis) (Acts 19:28)
664. 32,000 (Jdg 7:3)
665. The fruit of the vine (Matt 26:29)
666. Trumpets, pitchers and lamps (Jdg 7:15-22)
667. Philemon (Phm 1:10-11)
668. Macedonia (Acts 16-18)
669. Psalm 117 (Ps 117)
670. As a virtuous (worthy) woman (Ruth 3:11)
671. 12,000 (Rev 7:5-8)
672. Elijah (1 Ki 19:5)
673. Simon (the sorcerer) (Acts 8:18)
674. Wisdom (Pro 3:18)
675. Cousin / Sister's son (KJV) (Col 4:10)
676. ...bringeth his mother to shame (Pro 29:15)
677. Because he was a man of war (1 Chr 28:3)
678. Feet, hands and head (John 13:9)
679. Tongues of fire (Acts 2:3)
680. Feeding of the 5,000 and Jesus walks on water (John 6:1; 6:16)
681. Joshua (Josh 1:2)
682. Tent peg (Jdg 4:21)
683. Praise ye him, sun and moon, praise him, all ye stars of light (Ps 148:2-3)
684. Reuben (Gen 30:14)
685. Gold (Pro 16:16)
686. 1 Samuel (1 Sam 17)
687. They were afraid the Pharisees would put them out of the synagogue (John 12:42)
688. Repent: for the kingdom of heaven is at hand (Matt 4:17)
689. Pray for one another (Jam 5:16)
690. 110 (Josh 24:29)
691. Herod (the Great) (Matt 2:1)
692. Coriander (Num 11:7)
693. Andrew (John 6:8)
694. Count it all joy (Jam 1:2)
695. Man (Ps 103:15)
696. Horse (Rev 6)
697. Sparrows (Matt 10:29)
698. Terah (Gen 11:31)
699. In a dream (Matt 2:13)
700. Cast lots (Jon 1:7)

701. A band of men and officers (John 18:3)
702. Eight (2 Ki 22:1)
703. Nabal (1 Sam 25:3)
704. He was illegitimate and his brothers drove him out (Jdg 11:1-3)
705. Standing in synagogues and on street corners (Matt 6:5)
706. A lame man (Acts 14:8)
707. Grasshoppers (Num 13:33)
708. He claimed to be the Son of God (John 19:7)
709. Publican (tax collector) (Luke 18:10)
710. Simon (Peter) and Andrew (Matt 4:18-19)
711. Seventy (Jdg 8:30)
712. Third (Gen 1:11-13)
713. Cyprus (Acts 13:4)
714. They were covetous (loved money) (Luke 16:13-14)
715. Clothing (Jdg 14:12)
716. 120,000 (Jon 4:11)
717. A stone like a great millstone (Rev 18:21)
718. Despising God (1 Th 4:7-8)
719. In a basket down the city wall (Acts 9:23-25)
720. Foolishness (Pro 22:15)
721. The men of Gibeah (Jdg 19:15-28)
722. The rivers and fountains of waters became blood (Rev 16:4)
723. An onyx (Exo 28:9)
724. Theft (Josh 7:1)
725. Kish (1 Sam 14:51)
726. Lion, Bear, Leopard & Terrible beast (Dan 7:3-7)
727. Rubies (Pro 8:11)
728. Jewels and clothing (Exo 3:22)
729. Jesus (Mark 1:14)
730. Underwater creatures and birds (Gen 1:20-23)
731. Zaphnath-paaneah (Gen 41:45)
732. Made a whip (John 2:14)
733. You will sit on twelve thrones judging the twelve tribes of Israel (Matt 19:28)
734. Thousands upon thousands of angels (Rev 5:11-12)
735. Rebekah (Gen 24:14-19)
736. John (John 6:48)
737. 153 (John 21:11)
738. Micah (Mic 7:6)
739. Gibeon (Josh 9:3-6)
740. Priest (Luke 10:31)
741. Sent Timothy to encourage them (1 Th 3:1-2)
742. Call down fire from heaven (Luke 9:54)
743. Make one hair black or white (Matt 5:36)
744. Stars (Gen 1:14-18)
745. Pearls (Rev 21:21)
746. Psalm 90 (Ps 90:1)
747. Third (Gen 1:9-13)
748. Ten (1 Ki 11:31)
749. Simeon (Gen 42:24)
750. Twelve (Num 13:2-16)

751. Ostrich (Job 39:13-17)
752. Ishmael (Gen 21:21)
753. Righteousness (2 Pe 2:5)
754. Judah (Gen 29:35)
755. He who has many debts forgiven, loves the one who forgave him more than he who has few debts forgiven. (Luke 7:42-43)
756. 3,000 (Jdg 16:27)
757. Tychicus (Col 4:7-9)
758. Corinthians (2 Cor 6:17-18)
759. Malchus (John 18:10)
760. City gates (Jdg 16:3)
761. Philip (Acts 21:8)
762. Eutychus (Acts 20:9)
763. Elisha (2 Ki 5:10)
764. Tentmaker (Acts 18:2-3)
765. Almighty God (Gen 17:1)
766. Thou shall not commit adultery (Exo 20:14)
767. Three (Deut 4:41-43)
768. Manasseh (Gen 41:51)
769. Just / Godly / Blameless (Gen 6:9)
770. Two and a half (Josh 18:7)
771. Grandmother (2 Tim 1:5)
772. Levite (Luke 10:30-32)
773. Philippi (Acts 16:11-14)
774. Ammonites (Jdg 11:9-11)
775. Agabus (Acts 21:10-11)
776. Burned his house down while still inside it (1 Ki 16:18)
777. One pence (denarius) (Matt 20:2)
778. Phinehas' (1 Sam 4:19)
779. The poor (Luke 6:20)
780. Isaac ate of his venison (Gen 25:28)
781. Lambs (Lev 14:10)
782. Idle/disorderly brethren (2 Th 3:6)
783. The temptation of Jesus (Matt 4:6)
784. Mist went up from the earth (Gen 2:5-6)
785. Half (Luke 19:8)
786. Eighty-four (Luke 2:37)
787. Household gods / idols (Gen 31:19)
788. Psalm 58 (Ps 58:8)
789. In the beauty of holiness (Ps 96:9)
790. To gain understanding (Pro 4:1)
791. Lord will you at this time restore again the kingdom to Israel? (Acts 1:6)
792. Fish and honeycomb (Luke 24:42)
793. 110 (Gen 50:22)
794. Bethlehem (1 Sam 17:58)
795. In sanctification and honor (1 Th 4:4)
796. Thirty (Jdg 14:11)
797. Three (Gen 8:8-12)
798. Trumpets and cymbals (Ezr 3:10)
799. Twelve (Hos 1:1 - Mal 4:6)
800. Fifth (Exo 20:12)

Answers - Section Q

801. A man clothed in linen (Dan 10:5)
802. Benjamin (Jdg 20)
803. Crispus, Gaius and the household of Stephanas (1 Cor 1:14-16)
804. Gamaliel (Acts 5:34-39)
805. Mountains (Song 4:8)
806. Like a bride (Rev 21:2)
807. Salem (Gen 14:18, Heb 7:1)
808. Jeroboam II (2 Ki 14:23)
809. First (John 20:1)
810. Philippi (Acts 16:12)
811. Obadiah (Oba 1:1-21)
812. Blessed are the poor in spirit for theirs is the kingdom of heaven (Matt 5:3)
813. Sea of Tiberias (Galilee) (John 6:1; 21:1)
814. It doesn't say (Matt 2:1-12)
815. Samaria (Acts 8:12)
816. He was baptized (Acts 9:18)
817. Zarephath (1 Ki 17:9-23)
818. Samuel (1 Sam 15:22)
819. Bezaleel (Exo 31:2-3)
820. Ahijah (1 Ki 11:30-31)
821. Bread and wine (Gen 14:18)
822. Disputing who was the greatest disciple (Luke 22:24-30)
823. Hezekiah (2 Ki 18:9-12)
824. Locusts (Rev 9:1-4)
825. Myrtle (Zec 1:8)
826. Eight years (Jdg 12:13-14)
827. Seventy (Exo 15:27)
828. Four (Gen 2:10)
829. Elymas (Bar-Jesus) (Acts 13:8)
830. An ephah of barley (Ruth 2:17)
831. Joab (2 Sam 14:22)
832. In a candlestick (Luke 11:33)
833. A tree of life (Pro 15:4)
834. A well of Bethlehem (2 Sam 23:15-16)
835. Purim (Est 9:24-26)
836. Machpelah (Gen 23:19)
837. Egypt (1 Ki 10:28)
838. Calming of the storm (Mark 4:39 - 5:2)
839. To keep them separate as they were shepherds, which were an abomination to the Egyptians (Gen 46:34)
840. Haggai (Hag 2:4)
841. Philippi (1 Th 2:2)
842. Timothy (Acts 16:2)
843. The Spirit, the water and the blood (1 Jn 5:8)
844. By the fruit of his mouth (Pro 18:20)
845. Stalks of flax (Josh 2:6)
846. Three years (Acts 20:31)
847. John (John 1:1 - 21:25)
848. Pleasures for evermore (Ps 16:11)
849. Isaiah (Isa 20:2-3)
850. Sons of Jacob (Gen 34:13)

Answers - Section R

851. Mercurius (Hermes) (Acts 14:12)
852. It became as black as sackcloth (of hair) (Rev 6:12)
853. Faith and love (1 Th 5:8)
854. Horses (Deut 17:14-16)
855. Frogs (Rev 16:13)
856. 600 (Gen 7:6)
857. Rams (Exo 25:3-5)
858. Lemuel (Pro 31:1)
859. Abib (Deut 16:1)
860. The Ancient of Days (Dan 7:9)
861. Treasurer (Acts 8:27)
862. With singing (Ps 100:2)
863. 300 (1 Ki 11:3)
864. Threw a piece of wood into the water (Exo 15:23-25)
865. They were not ashamed (Gen 2:25)
866. Jehu (2 Ki 10:18-28)
867. Almond blossom (Exo 25:33)
868. They were chosen to fight against the Midianites (Jdg 7:5-7)
869. Five (Ps 1; 43; 73; 90; 107)
870. 127 years (Gen 23:1)
871. The coming of the Messiah (Dan 9:20-27)
872. Asher (Luke 2:36)
873. Girdle (belt) (Acts 21:11)
874. Evil men (Ps 140:1-3)
875. Annas (John 18:13)
876. Barnabas (Acts 13:4)
877. House of Israel (Matt 10:5-6)
878. On Earth (Rev 5:10)
879. Ishmaelites (Gen 37:28)
880. The sick (Jam 5:15)
881. Valley of Sorek (Jdg 16:4)
882. Onesiphorus (2 Tim 1:16)
883. Ten (Ruth 4:2)
884. It will sprout again (Job 14:7)
885. Trees for meat (Deut 20:19-20)
886. A young goat and some unleavened bread (Jdg 6:19)
887. Malta (Acts 28:1)
888. A crown (Pro 12:4)
889. Dan (Jdg 13:25)
890. Numbers (Num 22:22-35)
891. The Songs of Degrees (or Ascents) (Ps 120 - 134)
892. Butler (Gen 42:32-36)
893. God's creation (1 Tim 4:5)
894. A scorpion (Luke 11:12)
895. He had gone to Bethlehem for a family gathering (1 Sam 20:6)
896. Machpelah (Gen 50:12-13)
897. 350 years (Gen 9:28)
898. Silvanus (1 Th 1:1)
899. 147 (Gen 47:28)
900. A living dog (Ecc 9:4)

Answers - Section S

901. Sixth (Exo 9:8)
902. Corinth (Acts 18:1-5)
903. Elkanah (1 Sam 1:8)
904. His groanings (roarings) (Job 3:24)
905. Apples (Pro 25:11)
906. Jesus and the disciples celebrating Passover (Matt 26:30)
907. Ashkelon (Jdg 14:19)
908. Darius (Ezr 6:15)
909. Feet (1 Ki 15:23)
910. Zadok (1 Ki 1:39)
911. Father of Lights (Jam 1:17)
912. Philip (John 14:8)
913. Destroyed the rest of the royal family (2 Ki 11:1)
914. Og (Deut 3:11)
915. Paul (Acts 19:12)
916. He felt ill and weak (Dan 10:8)
917. Ezekiel (Eze 3:2)
918. Julius (Acts 27:1)
919. Ecclesiastes (Ecc 10:1)
920. Gravel (Pro 20:17)
921. A thirty foot flying roll (Zec 5:1-4)
922. Thirteen years (1 Ki 7:1)
923. Ai (Josh 7:5-12)
924. Fifty (Luke 7:41)
925. Aeneas (Acts 9:33)
926. Eighty-six years (Gen 16:16)
927. Seventy (2 Sam 5:4)
928. 300 cubits / 450 feet (Gen 6:15)
929. Two years (Acts 19:10)
930. Confusion and every evil work (Jam 3:16)
931. Joseph of Arimathea (Mark 15:43)
932. Tenth (Exo 20:17)
933. They must eat it on the day it is offered. (Lev 7:15; 22:30)
934. Zebulun (Gen 49:13)
935. Judgment, mercy, and faith (Matt 23:23)
936. Sihon (Deut 2:30; Jdg 11:19-20)
937. Bringing the ark back to Jerusalem (1 Chr 15-16)
938. Ninth (Exo 20:16)
939. Jupiter (Zeus) (Acts 14:12)
940. Two (Dan 8:3)
941. Colosse (Col 4:9; Phm 1:12)
942. Twin (John 11:16 / Strongs G1324)
943. Cyrus (Ezr 1:1-3)
944. Figs (2 Ki 20:7)
945. Elisha (2 Ki 6:17)
946. Seventeen (Jer 32:9)
947. Goats (Song 4:1)
948. Cain's fruit of the ground (Gen 4:3)
949. Those that do God's commandments (Rev 22:14)
950. Silver (Pro 10:20)

Answers - Section T

951. Dan, Asher, Naphtali (Num 2:25-29)
952. Berea (Acts 17:10)
953. 1,100 (Jdg 16:5)
954. Summer (Matt 24:32)
955. By lying (Pro 21:6)
956. Over the hole of a snake (Isa 11:8)
957. Deborah (Rebekah's nurse) (Gen 35:8)
958. Blue (Exo 28:31)
959. The Thessalonians (2 Th 1:3)
960. Ammon (Jer 49:1)
961. Lystra (Acts 14:8-12)
962. Prevails with God (Gen 32:28)
963. Build a guard rail around the roof (Deut 22:8)
964. Hosea (Hos 11:1)
965. Imagine evil (Pro 12:20)
966. Psalms (Mark 12:10; Ps 118:22)
967. Miletum (Miletus) (2 Tim 4:20)
968. A wall fell on them (1 Ki 20:30)
969. 666 talents (1 Ki 10:14)
970. James (Jam 1:1)
971. Benhadad (2 Ki 8:15)
972. A third (Deut 21:17; Luke 15:12)
973. Salt (2 Ki 2:21)
974. A cattle prod (ox goad) (Jdg 3:31)
975. Gad (Deut 4:43)
976. God has taken his power and commenced his reign (Rev 11:17)
977. His lawgiver (royal scepter) (Ps 60:7)
978. Bats (Isa 2:20)
979. Anna the Prophetess (Luke 2:36-38)
980. Two years and under (Matt 2:16)
981. The wicked (Ps 37:35)
982. Lydda (Acts 9:32-33)
983. Gihon (1 Ki 1:38)
984. Annas (Luke 3:2; John 18:13)
985. Rufus' (Rom 16:13)
986. Psalm 2 (Acts 13:33; Ps 2:7)
987. A parable (Pro 26:7)
988. With honor (1 Pe 3:7)
989. Isaac (Gen 26:1-7)
990. Because of the judgments of the Lord (Ps 48:11; 97:8)
991. 400 (Gen 23:16)
992. A Hittite (Eze 16:3)
993. One of the Scribes (Mark 12:28-34)
994. Archelaus (Matt 2:22)
995. Appii forum (Acts 28:15)
996. A pig's snout (Pro 11:22)
997. High father / Father of heights (Gen 17:5 / Strong's H87)
998. Nineteen (1 Chr 3:1-9)
999. The unthankful and the evil (Luke 6:35)
1000. Forty-eight (Josh 21:41)
1001. Jacob (Luke 1:33)

Printed in Great Britain
by Amazon